AMERICA AND EUROPE
AFTER 9/11 AND IRAQ

AMERICA AND EUROPE AFTER 9/11 AND IRAQ

The Great Divide

SARWAR A. KASHMERI

FOREWORD BY THEODORE ROOSEVELT IV

PRAEGER SECURITY INTERNATIONAL
Westport, Connecticut • London

Library of Congress Cataloging-in-Publication Data

Kashmeri, Sarwar A.
America and Europe after 9/11 and Iraq : the great divide / Sarwar A. Kashmeri.
p.   cm.
Includes bibliographical references and index.
ISBN 0–275–99301–9 (alk. paper)
1. Europe–Foreign relations–United States.   2. United States–Foreign
relations–Europe.   3. Europe–Foreign relations–21st century.   4. United States–
Foreign relations–2001–   I. Title.   II. Title: America and Europe after nine-eleven
and Iraq.   III. Title: America and Europe after September 11 and Iraq.
D2025.5.U64K37   2007
327.7304—dc22   2006028570

British Library Cataloguing in Publication Data is available.

Library of Congress Catalog Card Number: 2006028570
ISBN13: 978–0–275–99301–6
ISBN: 0–275–99301–9

First published in 2007

Praeger Security International, 88 Post Road West, Westport, CT 06881
An imprint of Greenwood Publishing Group, Inc.
www.praeger.com

Printed in the United States of America

The paper used in this book complies with the
Permanent Paper Standard issued by the National
Information Standards Organization (Z39.48–1984).

10   9   8   7   6   5   4   3   2   1

To Professor James Chace,
historian, writer, teacher, and raconteur
extraordinaire—whose life was tragically cut short on
October 8, 2004—for his many thoughtful, inspiring,
and at times provocative suggestions.

Contents

Foreword

The modern Atlantic Alliance was conceived and solidified during the horrors of World War II. It was not an easy alliance. The British thought the Americans were amateurs not prepared to take on the seasoned German army. While this was certainly true in the early years, the Americans deeply resented the thought that they were unfit to fight. Across the ocean, the British did not trust the French, and the French did not trust the British. Complicating the situation further, the Alliance included the Soviet Union, which complained that it was carrying the heaviest burden in the fight against the Nazis.

Though Winston Churchill and Franklin D. Roosevelt had a close personal relationship, the cohesiveness of the alliance was due in large part to the understanding and skilled leadership of General Dwight D. Eisenhower. Shared values aside, Eisenhower knew that a strong transatlantic alliance was one of the most important tools the United States had to defeat Nazi Germany. In the midst of uncertainty and in the face of formidable foes, Eisenhower experienced firsthand how hard it was to maintain the Alliance but also saw clearly that the benefits far outweighed the costs.

In the wake of World War II, the political leadership of the United States recognized the challenge posed by the Soviet Union and began to reconsider how World War II institutions and allies could take on a new role. Like World War II, the Cold War required partnership and cooperation with our allies across the Atlantic. Transatlantic ties were expanded to include West Germany, and our common economic interests were formally acknowledged through the Bretton Woods agreement of 1949, which created the World Bank, the International Monetary Fund, the United Nations, and GATT, the predecessor to the World Trade Organization. The common military interests of Europe and the United States were represented by NATO. These institutions worked in concert to help a devastated Europe recover economically, integrate itself politically, and protect itself militarily.

As the Cold War developed, the policy community on both sides of the Atlantic had to continue to rethink how best to manage the Alliance. The most valuable response came from the brilliant George Kennan, who formulated his famous strategy of containment. Kennan's basic approach was to avoid a direct military confrontation and limit Soviet expansion. This required unprecedented cooperation and commitment between the United States and our Western allies. The fall of the Berlin Wall in 1989 and the subsequent collapse of the Soviet Union proved the validity of Kennan's approach and highlighted the value of a strong transatlantic community. Together, the Atlantic Alliance had succeeded at staving off another major war on the continent, had played an important part in transforming a divided Europe into a unified one, and had taken a devastated economy and turned it into America's most important trading partner.

With the demise of the Soviet Union, many Americans began to focus on the costs of the Alliance and tended to direct their attention away from the benefits of strong transatlantic ties. Sarwar Kashmeri explains clearly in his book how most American observers overlooked the political and economic dimensions of an integrated Europe and how the transformation of Europe into a strong community with independent political and economic interests was generally not recognized or appreciated on this side of the Atlantic. Without the threat of the Soviet Union, the value of the Alliance has been overlooked, and it has ultimately been weakened.

Despite this trend, the threats that the West faces today require a strong Atlantic Alliance more than ever. As former National Security Advisor Zbigniew Brzezinski points out in an article for the *American Interest* in autumn 2005, the Internet, television, and radio have resulted in instantaneous communication throughout the world and have helped facilitate a "political awakening unprecedented in scope and intensity, with the result that the politics of populism are transforming the politics of power." Aggrieved communities, particularly Muslims in their traditional homelands and across Europe, have resorted to contemptible attacks on civilians. The response in the United States has been to declare the "War on Terror." This term is misleading; we are actually in a conflict with "radical Islam" that has successfully leveraged America's unilateralism, perceived or otherwise, into growing resistance throughout the Muslim world.

Just as the Alliance needed to be reinvented after World War II to confront the challenges of the Cold War, the Alliance must be rethought once again to meet the threats posed by an amorphous, stateless, and global conflict with radical Islam. As Richard Haas points out in his recent book *The Opportunity*, "Integration is the natural successor to containment." Rather than seeing the Atlantic Alliance as a relic of the late twentieth century, it should be seen as a crucial partnership in addressing the difficulties we face.

This conflict will not be successfully won if we resort primarily to military measures, which are most effective against sovereign states but are relatively ineffective against nonstate actors and insurgencies. Globalization has eroded the power and legitimacy of sovereign states. The flow of capital across borders limits control of currencies, the ability of companies to outsource manufacturing impacts employment, and the increasing volume of cross-border trade exposes companies to greater competition in their domestic markets. But part and parcel of these complications is globalization's ability to increase flows of information, trade, capital, and the broadened opportunities for bonds between nations. Recognition of these links and their importance to economic growth and to political stability provide the opportunity to build powerful alliances to help protect shared interests and common values.

As Eisenhower saw firsthand, great alliances require nurturing and commitment to succeed. Emphasizing the importance of the Atlantic Alliance, with its shared history, common culture, and dedication to democratic values is an obvious place to begin in building the relationships that the United States will need if it wants to continue to play the historical role it has as a benign world leader.

Theodore Roosevelt IV

Preface

My interest in the strategic implications of the European Union began during the late 1990s, when I headed up a financial systems integration company that specialized in installing multicurrency accounting systems. Most of its American multinational clients had offices in Europe, where the unprecedented replacement of eleven European currencies with the euro was a few short months away. The question that was uppermost on the minds of the companies' chief financial officers was the impact of this transition on their accounting practices and systems. As I got deeper into the issues, it struck me that the technical problems related to the euro's introduction were relatively straightforward. It was the strategic sweep of the ongoing European integration, now about to be supercharged by the euro, that was the real news. A borderless Europe with its new common currency was about to alter the rules for European marketing, cross-border financing, treasury management, marketing, pricing, and a host of other issues that constitute the operational heart of any business's strategic plan.

American businesses were soon going to face a whole new set of opportunities and threats in Europe. I also discovered that very few of them were aware of this sea change and prepared to deal with it. So I decided to organize a series of high-level conferences to explain the business impact of the euro to American companies. These events gave me an opportunity to refine my thoughts and discuss Europe's transformation with financial executives and corporate and government leaders on both sides of the Atlantic.

It was one of these conferences, held at the State Department in Washington, DC, that got me thinking about the foreign policy aspects of a rapidly integrating Europe. A number of officials from the Clinton administration took the time to participate, and these contacts further sharpened my understanding of the business and political issues and their impact on the transatlantic alliance.

In April 2003, the Foreign Policy Association—the country's oldest bipartisan organization dedicated to educating Americans about foreign policy—and my then company, ebizChronicle.com, Inc., hosted a conference at Ditchley, UK, to explore the impact of the European Union on the transatlantic alliance. The American-led invasion of Iraq was barely four weeks old when we met at the eighteenth-century Elizabethan Manor where these conferences are held. The very public spat between Europeans and Americans during the lead-up to the war had been front-page news for months and had opened up a deep rift between the erstwhile allies. The weekend confirmed my growing feeling that the causes of the present rift are much deeper and more permanent than meet the eye. I had been preparing a brief article on this point, but the frank (and I might add rather energetic) off-the-record exchange at Ditchley inspired me to expand my treatment into the present book. The participants at this conference approved the release of an "Organizers' Note," which is included in this volume as Appendix A.

The United States and Europe, I believe, have arrived at a critical crossroad, and the path they choose will determine whether or not the alliance survives. Corporations faced with a decision that puts their company's survival at risk organize strategy sessions of their most experienced executives and advisors to help in charting the company's future. With so much at stake, I asked myself, why not use the same technique in this instance? Why not talk to eminent people with substantial expertise and hands-on experience in managing various aspects of the alliance and use their expertise to understand better the alliance's decayed state and to help chart a future for it? So I contacted a number of business, government, and armed forces leaders and found they were very concerned about the alliance's future and, crucially, quite willing to speak to me on the record. (In order to accommodate his busy schedule, former President George H. W. Bush asked whether we could do a question-and-answer via e-mail, which we did; all the rest of the interviews were conducted in person.) The conversations took place over a one-year period from February 2003 to February 2004. During May 2006 I met again with Senator Hagel and General Scowcroft to clarify some of our discussion further.

The interlocutors were:

George H. W. Bush	41st President of the United States
John Major	Former Prime Minister of the United Kingdom
James A. Baker, III	Former U.S. Secretary of the Treasury and Secretary of State
Wesley K. Clark	General, U.S. Army (Ret.) and former Supreme Allied Commander, Europe
Chuck Hagel	United States Senator (R), Nebraska
Hugo Paemen	Former ambassador of the European Union to the United States
Ana de Palacio	Former foreign minister of Spain
Brent Scowcroft	Former National Security Advisor
Paul Volcker	Former chairman, Federal Reserve Bank
Caspar Weinberger	Former chairman of *Forbes*; former Secretary of Defense

I used these one-on-one conversations to refine my ideas and conclusions. Where appropriate, direct quotations from these conversations are used to illuminate my narrative. If one of the leaders mentioned above is quoted in this book without a citation, the reader can assume it is a direct quote from our conversations.

There is no question that my interlocutors were enormously helpful as sources of first-hand information. They inspired me. But the conclusions I came to are entirely my own, and it would be a mistake to link them to any particular interlocutor.

Acknowledgments

First and foremost I would like to acknowledge the kindness of the ten leaders who agreed to converse with me for this book. Each of them opened a unique window for me into that rarified world at the pinnacle of power. These forthright conversations were the building blocks for my book. To each of them I owe very special thanks.

When I was first thinking about this book, I conceived it to be a collection of reminiscences and projections on the future of the transatlantic alliance by each one of my interlocutors. During a conversation with General Brent Scowcroft, he asked how I intended to write this book, and when I told him, Scowcroft looked at me with despair and said, "I hope not. You should tell your story and use us for backup material." If you have had the good fortune (or perhaps not such good fortune!) of sitting across the table from Scowcroft when he advises you to do something, you know how difficult it is to do otherwise. And that's how the book came to be what it is now. So, thank you, General!

A special thanks is also due Peter Jay, former British ambassador to the United States. At a conference that was held at Ditchley, UK, in December 2002—as the transatlantic debate on the wisdom and legality of invading Iraq was reaching boiling point—Peter and I stepped away from the luncheon crowd and spent an hour discussing the past, present, and future of the alliance. More accurately, I mostly listened while Peter spoke. His passionate and experienced discourse put a lot of the thoughts that had been rumbling through my head into focus; Peter is another reason this book came to be.

Sir Nigel Broomfield, the former Director of Ditchley, served as an early guide and soundboard for this book and offered encouragement when I most needed it.

My businessman's inquisitiveness and interest in American foreign policy has been nurtured and encouraged over the years by Noel Lateef, president of the Foreign Policy Association. I want to acknowledge his friendship and guidance. The FPA is a unique bipartisan organization dedicated to explaining the conduct of foreign policy to Americans, a job it has been doing with skill for almost a century. Never has the need for the excellent work its dedicated staff produces been more important than it is today.

Jim McGrath worked as a speechwriter for President George H. W. Bush during his White House years, and still does. I came to know Jim when he called me for some help in creating a speech that his boss delivered at a Union League Club dinner at which I officiated. We have been friends since. He let me borrow freely of his time when I was getting started with my book and offered incisive encouragement and critique. Thank you, Jim.

My interest in the European Union and the euro—then the EU's biggest work-in-progress—began in the late 1990s, when information on these topics was in embarrassingly short supply from the American media. The ebullient Wouter Wilton, then in charge of the European Commission's Press Office in New York, and his hard-working and widely read associate, Christopher Matthews, took me under their wings and ensured a regular and steady supply of information and experts headed my way. New Yorkers pride themselves in their networking skills, but Wouter is in a class by himself!

My friend, Thomas Twetten, who had a long and distinguished CIA career was gracious enough to read the manuscript and offer some excellent suggestions that included his catching a major omission. With his editor's eye for detail, Tom's tenure in the Agency must have produced scores of agents who went on to writing careers!

My good friend Anna Typrowicz, who is a professional editor, proofed and copyedited the manuscript before I sent it to Praeger. She did this in record time, and I shudder to think what it would have looked like had she not fit it into her busy schedule.

My brother Zuhair Kashmeri, one of Canada's noted journalists and writers who is two books ahead of me, was an inspiration and guide. And my wife, Deborah, was the model of patience over the two years that this book was written. In many ways that only she will understand, I owe her a lot.

I'd been told how difficult it is to sell that first book. Hearing it and experiencing it are two different things. There is no doubt in my mind that without the tenacious, creative, and unrelenting efforts of my agent, Sally van Haitsma of the Castiglia Literary Agency, this book would not be. So thank you, Sally and Julie Castiglia.

My involvement in the European-American relationship began almost ten years ago, and the thoughts distilled here were formed in countless conversations with businessmen, politicians, writers, journalists, involved citizens, and especially taxi drivers (who seem closer to being the fount of accurate political information than anyone else) on both sides of the Atlantic. It is impossible to thank them all, but I can at least acknowledge their influence. Hilary Claggett, my editor at Praeger, is the other reason this book sees the light of day. She made this novice writer feel at ease.

Sarwar A. Kashmeri
Reading, Vermont
August 1, 2006

Introduction

It was an alliance the likes of which had rarely been seen before: Europeans, Arabs, and Americans, fighting together under an American general to defeat an Arab dictator. The year was 1991, and President George H. W. Bush had put this coalition together, after getting approval from the United Nations, to roll Saddam Hussein's invading armies from Kuwait. The military operation turned out to be spectacularly successful. The invaders were thrown out and the Iraqi military defeated in a matter of days. The allies basked in glory and wrote out checks to pay America for its operating expenses. Not since World War II had America's reputation for working with its allies and doing what is right been so clearly on display.

In 2003 the United States went to war again with another coalition against Saddam Hussein. Under the presidency of President George W. Bush, the former president's son, the United States invaded Iraq without the approval of the United Nations. No major Arab country joined this alliance; none of America's major European allies, except Britain, fought on America's side. Three years and billions of dollars later, America continues to expend its human and financial capital, and the situation appears increasingly desperate every day.

In only one respect has this invasion of Iraq achieved total success—in worsening the rupture of the transatlantic alliance.

If the crack in this erstwhile rock-solid alliance had been widening for some time, the Iraqi crisis brought it to the breaking point. The transatlantic bloodletting that took place during the Iraqi discussions within the United Nations Security Council was sobering for the insight it provided into the extent of damage that had already been done to the European-American relationship. The alliance that just a few years earlier had forced an end to the Soviet Empire without firing a shot, and freed millions of people from brutal tyranny, now appeared on the verge of disintegrating.

Conventional wisdom has it that the European-American rift over the Iraqi war will heal itself, as others did before it. Given time, a change in personalities, and a more multilateral tone to American foreign policy, the alliance will come roaring back. I submit that this will not happen. This European-American rift is fundamentally different from previous ones, and the alliance–created in 1949–is no longer suited to today's geopolitical realities. In my opinion, if a new alliance is not negotiated between Europe and the United States, there will not be a Western alliance in the future. Were this to happen, it would be a tragedy. The new security challenges of the twenty-first century, the limitations to American power that are now evident from its tragically mismanaged invasion of Iraq, and the complementary strengths that Europe and America bring to the table, call out for a strong transatlantic alliance. And in turn, these security challenges offer opportunities to forge an alliance tailored for the new century's geopolitical realities. These conclusions were reinforced by private conversations with ten influential leaders from both sides of the Atlantic.

I'd like to offer an alternative view of American foreign policy, one that is opposed to its present direction under the influence of the transformationalists and neoconservatives whose influence continues to direct the current administration's foreign policy. This alternative view is shared by a large number of Republicans and Democrats and could well form the basis for a return to bipartisan policymaking and the reorientation of American foreign policy towards a new transatlantic alliance.

Neoconservatives, who are mainly Republicans, celebrate short-term obstacles on the road to European integration and want the United States to help deepen the splits in European ranks. They maintain that a commercially and politically integrated Europe is not in America's best interest, and they would like to see an American policy that forces European governments to choose between Paris and Washington. To this end, the neoconservatives support the Europhobic lobby in Britain to encourage Britain's strategic independence.[1] Their equally conservative but clearer-thinking Republican brethren disapprove of this policy. Instead, these Republicans believe that a policy of trying to divide the Europeans, if adopted by the United States, will doom the transatlantic alliance, and this in turn will damage America's long-term security and commercial interests.

However, I also contend that the continuing schism within the Republican Party's foreign policy ranks, and the embedded and continuing influence of the neoconservative doctrine on the country's foreign policy, do not bode well for the alliance's future.

The current downward spiral of the transatlantic relationship should be of real concern to Americans for three main reasons.

First, the transatlantic divide's timing could not be more damaging as Europe continues to build the European Union, which has emerged as a potential rival to America's global supremacy. Former President George H. W. Bush recognized this clearly. "The Europeans are in the process of trying to forge a common understanding about security and foreign policy. It's important for the United States to participate in the dialogue from the beginning—which will ensure that America is treated as the ally that it is and not a competitor," he told me. Do we really want to disengage from the Europeans at this crucial time?

Second, Europe is the United States' most natural ally in the fight against terrorism. Both share a common idea of an individual's place in society and his or her relationship to government; the concepts of liberal democracy and liberty are woven into the fabric of the United States and the European Union. Facing a future scarred by the general availability of destructive technologies and a growing clash between competing visions of statehood, an alliance can substantially increase the odds that freedom will prevail.

It is also worth recalling that as global economies recover from the recent downturn, it is Asia's galloping growth, not Europe's anemic economic performance, that supports America's own economic recovery. American businessmen, policy makers, and geopolitical analysts increasingly look East, not West, to sustain their companies. Business support for the European cause might be more fragile than it seems.

I contend that European integration, even though it has been going on for fifty years, is barely understood in the United States. I first realized this a decade ago when Europeans were establishing the timeline to introduce their single currency while we in the United States were still arguing among ourselves as to whether the euro would ever be launched. The Germans give up their mighty deutschemark? The French ditch their cherished franc? Never! It had simply never registered on many American business and government leaders that European states had been giving up pieces of their sovereignty for almost fifty years to create the European Union, and that France, Germany, Spain, and Italy—representing over 75 percent of the continental European economies[2]—had *already* signed a treaty with eight other countries to establish the euro.

There was, I felt, a continuing belief in America that the European Union is unimportant because the Europeans will never create anything like a "United States of Europe." This conviction flew in the face of fifty years of steady and tangible accomplishments toward an ever closer and tighter European Union, as member countries ceded increasing amounts of sovereignty to it. There is not a sufficient appreciation in America for an increased feeling of being European among Italians and Germans and Irish and, yes, even the British.

Americans who believe that Europe is now divided into "old Europe" and "new Europe" manifest this attitude. Yes, there were countries that broke European ranks and took the American side in the Iraqi war, but these divisions, in my opinion, are short-term tactical moves that will ultimately be negotiated away for the cause of European integration. In a similar vein, I do not agree with those who view the recent failure of Europeans to achieve consensus on a constitution for the European Union as a fatal setback. European countries have an age-old tradition of confronting each other, and such behavior is not something easily sur-mounted in fifty years. It is a miracle the Europeans have managed to get to where they are today, bearing in mind where they started from.

I use the Iraqi war as a prism to break out the reasons why the current rift is fundamentally different from previous ones. The end of the Cold War is an important piece of the puzzle, but not the only one.

Other reasons were previously buried because of the threat posed by the Soviet Union during the Cold War. These include cultural differ-ences, religious attitudes, differing interpretations of the phrase "war on terrorism," structural differences within the European Union and a lead-ership struggle within its ranks, lack of understanding of the influence of the American West on United States foreign policy, and differing per-ceptions of what constitutes a "threat."

But don't the common values and interests and NATO ensure the alliance will ultimately prevail? Perhaps, but not necessarily. In our conversation Paul Volcker observed that although he thought Americans and Europeans shared a lot of values, he was not sure that prevented us from having another conflict. He only half mischievously pointed out that one could have said the same about the Germans and French before World War II.

In reality, a powerful new European political entity, with foreign pol-icy and security priorities different from those of the United States, has arrived. America, however, still forges its foreign policy toward Europe on the basis of Cold War realities. Both Republicans and Democrats are complicit in this behavior, and NATO is a prime example of the biparti-san disconnect. NATO is touted as the very symbol of the alliance, when its main reason for existence—the Soviet threat to Europe—is gone, and as an American-led entity, it is now increasingly unacceptable to the Euro-peans. Defense Secretary Rumsfeld's assertion of NATO's role as the alli-ance's linchpin at the February 2005 Munich Security Conference drew a dismissive response from Chancellor Schroeder of Germany, who made it clear that NATO was no longer the primary venue where trans-atlantic partners discuss and coordinate security strategy.

I happen to be an unshakable supporter of and believer in the transatlantic alliance—in its broadest sense as an European-American relationship, not just an Anglo-American one, nor as a synonym for NATO. Is there a constructive agenda for rebuilding the alliance going forward? An agenda to bind Europe and America together again in the same way as the threat from the Soviet Union bound the alliance during the Cold War? My answer is, yes there is, and I present my thoughts for rebuilding the alliance.

My proposal is for the United States and Europe to take the initiative to develop new global rules of engagement and participate in a serious dialogue on the use of force—when is it justified and how should it be used. America and Europe do not, any longer, share the same vision about this. I believe America should take the initiative to start this dialogue, and make it clear to the Europeans that they will sit as equals across the table.

I also propose that America end its existing foreign policy tilt towards Britain. The only "special relationship" that matters, in my opinion, is the one between the United States and the European Union. The misadventure in Iraq might never have been launched without the Blair government's self-serving and unequivocal support for the invasion.

Another recommendation is for Europe and the United States to engage jointly in a wide range of projects focused on attacking the root causes of poverty, illiteracy, and disease around the world and to jumpstart education programs through that vast crescent that sweeps from the Mediterranean to the borders of China. These projects will also go a long way to strengthen mutual understanding between the West and the Islamic world.

Europe and America also need to begin immediately the work of ending the huge inequalities that exist between Western and developing countries. Neither side can successfully do this alone.

The proposals represent a substantial agenda that will require long-term engagement between the alliance partners at the highest level for many years—which is exactly what the alliance needs now.

Lord Palmerston, the plain-speaking nineteenth-century Prime Minister of England, famously observed that countries have no permanent friends, just permanent interests.[3] Besides their business ties, Europe and America have few common interests now. The challenges of the new century require that the erstwhile allies coalesce around a core set of common interests and leverage their considerable combined resources and skills to create a new transatlantic alliance in order to manage these challenges over the next fifty years as skillfully as they managed the challenges of the last fifty.

CHAPTER ONE

This Rift Is Different

I really think that the French-British leadership tussle was at the heart of this rift.
—*General Brent Scowcroft, former National Security Advisor*

"For Old Friends, Iraq Crisis Bares a Deep Rift in Views," headlined the *New York Times* on February 11, 2003. "Now something deep and fundamental in the different views of Europe and the United States seems to have been brought to the surface by the Iraqi crisis," the article said. "How did transatlantic relations which were so good recently, get so bad so quickly?" it asked.[1] How indeed? It was a question many people in Europe and America had been asking themselves as the Iraqi drama unfolded.

Had not the conventional wisdom been that, at the end of the day, Europe and America have the same basic values and interests? No matter what, went this line of thinking, in the end, the decades-old alliance always cycles back to its happy and stable state of equilibrium. Tiffs are natural in relationships between friendly states, but they do not last very long, because differences between long-standing allies are transient, not "deep and fundamental" differences. But buried in the headline was another question: were there other forces at play that had changed the European-American alliance's nature, so that the old rules and assumptions did not apply any more?

Over its half-century of existence the alliance has experienced many rifts and bounced back from them. Just in the four years preceding the invasion, serious divisions had developed over the differing perceptions of such important issues as the establishment of the World Court at The

Hague, the Kyoto Treaty to limit greenhouse gases, and the unilateral American abrogation of the antiballistic missile treaty that had been signed with the Soviet Union, but they had not cut to the bone. The Iraqi war, however, appears to have changed everything and become a point of no return for the alliance, as when an axe strikes a seemingly solid piece of wood that instantly cracks open, revealing the decayed core inside.

Caspar Weinberger

In a conversation at New York's Union League Club a few weeks before the Iraqi war began, and as the transatlantic rift reached boiling-point, Caspar Weinberger, secretary of defense under President Ronald Reagan, reminded me that the alliance had faced very serious rifts before, and the behavior now on display was a characteristic of the European-American alliance. I had started my quest to gauge the nature of the transatlantic rift over Iraq with someone who had dealt with the Europeans during the greatest buildup of United States military strength since the Second World War and who had been at the center of moving the Soviet-American Cold War to its tipping point. I wanted him to help me place the current rift in perspective from his unique vantage point.

In Weinberger's experience in dealing with the Europeans, "Every time we concluded we had to do something difficult or something which involve[d] risk, perhaps even the risk of war, there was enormous imme-diate opposition," he told me. "The opposition was not based on [the belief that] what we were trying to do was wrong, but on the fact that there was too much risk, and that anything was better than war."

Weinberger, who died in March 2006, was then a sprightly 85, slightly stooped, but still razor-sharp in his thinking. He spoke in short sentences and seemed to put more substance into one sentence than many other people could put into paragraphs. I had learned to admire his sense of humor and friendly eyes. It would have been easy to underestimate him until one had experienced the steel that lay within.

He had been the unwavering rebuilder of America's armed forces during the Reagan years and oversaw $2 trillion worth of defense spend-ing. When he left office, America's military had been transformed to the most powerful fighting machine the world had ever seen. He continued to believe that it was wrong to assume that the whole aim of diplomacy was an agreement. "I always said the easiest thing you can get is an agreement," he said. "You can get an agreement in five or ten minutes, but the problem is you need to have some trust the person across the table will keep his word, and that is not always possible." To his admirers, it was this cold, hard-thinking and Weinberger's and President Reagan's unshakable belief that the "Cold War" had to be won, backed up by the might of America's new military, that had finally convinced the Soviet Union to throw in the towel, give up their aim of world domination, and implode. There was, however, another side to Weinberger's crusade to build the world's most effective military. It was captured in his obituary published by the *Washington Post* on Wednesday, March 29, 2006:

> Some thought it was incongruous that I did so much to build up our defenses but was reluctant to commit forces abroad. I did not arm to attack . . . We armed so that we could negotiate from strength, defend freedom and make war less likely.[2]

Weinberger told me about the 1979 decision to deploy intermediate-range ballistic missiles in Europe in order to counter the threat of the Soviet SS-20 nuclear missiles with which the Russians had targeted virtually every European capital city. "Europeans were convinced the United States was about to unleash nuclear war and destroy the world, [and it was] generating massive opposition," he said.

It was France that took the full brunt of the blows rained on the recalcitrant Europeans by the American administration during the lead-up to the Iraqi war, and France returned them in full measure. To most Americans it was inconceivable that France, an ally, had threatened to veto the second United Nations resolution on Iraq without even seeing it; this seemed to cross all boundaries of behavior by an ally. I asked Weinberger whether he could remember France doing anything like it before. He did. If France's behavior during the lead-up to the Iraq crisis was considered detrimental to the alliance from an American perspective, it was, in some ways worse during the 1980s.

Terrorist acts had then killed a number of people in Europe, including many American service men and women. After the United States had proof that Libyan intelligence was responsible for the terrorism, President Reagan decided to attack Libya. The United Kingdom immediately offered the use of its NATO bases, but France refused fly-over rights, forcing American planes to fly hundreds of miles out of the way. This required three or four air-to-air refueling operations, at night in total radio silence—a very dangerous procedure. "France's decision actually put our pilots' lives at risk and was totally inexcusable," Weinberger told me. It is hard to imagine a more serious charge against an ally.

But, after all the acrimony, fierce opposition, and debate engendered by the missile crisis of the 1970s and the attack on Libya of the 1980s, the alliance had come back together, gained in strength, and then gone on to achieve two spectacular successes. Aggressive and farsighted American diplomacy, coupled with a collaborative transatlantic strategy, ended the

Soviet Empire, reunited Germany, and set the stage for further growth of the vibrant commercial relationship that now exists between America and Europe.

If time had healed those deep wounds, is it not logical to assume that the present rift over Iraq will also dissipate with time, and the alliance will come roaring back? Or is the rift over Iraq different from the ones Weinberger spoke of? That, it seemed to me, was the critical question raised by the *New York Times* headline.

Brent Scowcroft

If there is a Renaissance personality on America's geopolitical stage it is Brent Scowcroft, National Security Advisor under President George H. W. Bush and one of that President's closest friends and advisers. Historian, strategist, statesman, Air Force general, writer, and professor (he taught Russian history at West Point), he is also one of the most accomplished and least pretentious members of the upper echelons of Washington's power elite. On the hot August 2003 day we met in his Washington, D.C., office, the building had lost all power and was without air conditioning, so a shirt-sleeved Scowcroft led me to the coffee shop around the corner for our interview. He was as genuinely comfortable in that nondescript booth as I had seen him in other, more genteel black-tie surroundings.

"Maybe it is the proximity," Scowcroft told me, "but I think this crisis is worse." There was no doubt in his mind that Europeans and Americans had had some fierce discussions and arguments during the Cold War, but they were within the framework of a common resistance to the Soviet Union. That was a powerful incentive to conclusion, and at the end of the debate both America and Europe would end up stronger. "We don't have that impetus to conclusion now because there is nothing that drives us to conclusion," he said.

The overriding common interest that helped the allies get over serious disagreements in the past is the Achilles heel of the present rift—that common interest was the Cold War, which does not exist any more. Not only is the Iraqi crisis more serious than past ones, but, Scowcroft believed, "It also illuminated a deeper core issue, which isn't about Iraq at all, but the competition between France and Britain for the leadership of the European Union." This competition is of critical importance to understanding the state of today's American-European relations.

Scowcroft believed that for some time the French have had the notion that, as long as the United States was in Europe, two consequences must follow: "Europe couldn't develop organically, and France couldn't lead Europe." As the Iraq debate unfolded, the French saw that European public opinion was *strongly* opposed to what America wanted to do in Iraq, and they thought this was their chance to get out ahead, lead European public opinion, and get the United States out of Europe. Before the Cold War ended, France would never have challenged the United States directly because of the Soviet Union. "And now there is no reason not to," Scowcroft said.

The British were on the other side of this European coin. The British were saying, in Scowcroft's words, "'Don't pay any attention to the French, we are the ones who can control the European Union—this 800-pound gorilla across the Atlantic—we are the natural leaders of Europe, we are the bridge between continental Europe and the United States.' I really think that [the French-British leadership tussle] was at the heart of this rift."

This description of the rift over Iraq as fundamentally different from past rifts because of the end of the Cold War, coupled with the forces and ripples unleashed by the emergence of the European Union, would recur throughout my conversations, even as other pieces of the puzzle fell into place.

Wesley Clark

Nothing exemplifies the transatlantic alliance as does the North Atlantic Treaty Organization. Scowcroft's belief that at its heart the current rift is really about the future leadership of the European Union was shared by General Wesley Clark, who, as Supreme Allied Commander in Europe, led NATO into battle during the Kosovo crisis—the only battle NATO has ever fought. It was not the most inspiring episode in NATO history. Geared to blocking and defeating a Soviet invasion of Europe, NATO found itself unprepared to deal with the politically infected conflict in the Balkans, against forces that, under other circumstances, would not have lasted an hour against it on the battlefield.

I was particularly interested in Clark's opinions, because he has experienced the alliance's strengths and weaknesses from a unique vantage point—that of a general who had to please multiple bosses (fifteen EU nations, NATO, and the United States) and win a war at the same time.

Clark and I spoke at the Regency Hotel in New York just a week before he announced his attempt to win the Democratic nomination for the 2004 Presidential elections. For the record, I left our meeting without any clue as to his intentions in this regard but with a healthy respect for his grasp of transatlantic issues and personalities, his engaging qualities as an interlocutor, and his sense of humor.

I found Clark, physically trim and precise in his language, engaging and even inspiring to talk to. His knowledge of post–World War II Europe is impressive. He is a scholar, soldier, raconteur, and business-man rolled into one, with a contagious sense of humor that acts as a release valve for the almost continuous high-powered responses that he is wont to give. At one point I asked Clark about his ideas on a positive agenda that would engage Americans and Europeans and alleviate the rift. "Go over and have breakfast with the Europeans," he advises his fel-low Americans. "You'll find them to be quite interesting, and you may be surprised and even like them."

Clark agrees with Scowcroft about this rift's seriousness and the underlying European leadership issues concerning France and the United Kingdom, but Clark takes them a few steps further.

"For France, especially, there are multiple leadership issues, world leadership issues," he told me. According to Clark, France has always taken a global view; it has possessions around the world, and it views its responsibilities and capabilities as global in scope even though it is smaller than the United States.

France believes it has a certain cultural and historic superiority in terms of finesse, in its ability to see problems and react and respond appropriately. It has for years dealt with peacekeeping in North and South Africa and, since Algeria,[3] has done quite well. "It inserts forces, it manipulates local elites, it rewards and punishes, it extracts, it re-inserts, it fights quiet wars—with professional soldiers and skilled diplomats—wars that slide under the nose of the French political system," Clark said. So, while there is no question in Clark's mind that the issue of French leader-ship of the European Union was an important element of the rift over Iraq, he wants to underscore that France also views itself as a global player with substantial political and commercial links to Iraq that in some cases go back a century. That role also contributed to the positions France took during the Iraq debates.

Clark's description of France's ability to deploy military power effec-tively is at odds with popular American impressions of the French as weak-kneed people who appear to disdain the exercise of military power and lack a competent military. Of course, this impression has no basis in reality, given, for instance, France's military contribution to the interna-tional peacekeeping force in Afghanistan, with French commandos con-ducting joint operations with American Special Forces along the Pakistan-Afghanistan border, not to mention France's sizable army and independent nuclear deterrent. But, coming as it did from a previous head of NATO, the observation seemed even more relevant.

On the other side of the English Channel, according to Clark, Prime Minister Tony Blair has always viewed the United Kingdom not just as a predominant military power in Europe but also as a cultural bridge between America and the continent of Europe. Clark believes that when and if the British prime minister raises his country's profile within the European Union and makes a grand entrance into Europe, it will not be on the basis of surrendering the United Kingdom's economic sovereignty by replacing the pound sterling with the euro but on the basis of providing military capabilities that are sufficiently robust to make the European Union a desirable security partner for the United States and one that would make America feel secure. This mission is poles apart from the French vision of an integrated Europe with its own armed forces that will provide a balance to America as the sole superpower and will add geopolitical balance in the world.

For all these reasons, Clark is convinced this rift is much more serious and complex than the previous ones, and he uses an analogy from economics to explain the nature of the rift and why it is taking place. Economic activity goes through a cycle of inflations and recessions as a part of the normal conduct of business. These cyclical recessions tend to be self-correcting, but every now and then there is a recession caused by extraordinary events. Such recessions cannot correct themselves and require strong corrective intervention, such as an immediate lowering of interest rates. If left to themselves, the recessions will just get worse and cause even further economic damage. "You have recessions and then you have structural recessions," Clark told me. "This is a structural problem, and in that sense it is different from previous rifts."

Although the subject of NATO and its continuing relevance will be explored in a later chapter, it is worth pointing out here that both Clark and Scowcroft believe the United States made a tragic mistake by refusing to include NATO in the coalition that fought the war in Afghanistan. After the attacks of September 11, 2001, the Europeans, through NATO, had stepped up to the plate and, for the first time ever, invoked NATO's Article 5, which in essence states that aggression against one NATO member is an aggression against all of them. NATO members then wanted to join the war against the Taliban in Afghanistan, but they were judged by the United States to be deficient in battle readiness and the technologies needed to conduct effective military operations; that they would be like an anchor—a burden that would have to be lugged into battle. NATO, an organization in which billions of dollars and endless amount of political capital had been invested, was left to watch on the sidelines. This, Clark maintained, was an unnecessary slight and a grave miscalculation. With the emergence of the European Union and its growing economic and military integration, "there is for Europe now a potential alternative to the alliance for the first time, and there is no Soviet Union pushing the two sides together," Clark said.

The effect on the alliance of not at least trying to use NATO is not trivial. Stop an American or a European on the street and ask them what the phrase "transatlantic alliance" means, and chances are the response will be "NATO." With the end of the Cold War, NATO is the only remaining forum where all of the alliance partners interact almost continuously. This "clubby" feeling, carefully nurtured over fifty years by generations of soldiers and statesmen, is a powerful generator of goodwill for both sides. In an unprecedented display of solidarity, on September 12, 2001–just one day after the attacks of September 11–NATO, acting under its Article 5 authorization, authorized the dispatch of five NATO airborne surveillance planes and two hundred military personnel to help patrol the United States' East Coast, in a marginally useful but highly symbolic demonstration of transatlantic solidarity. In less than a month these NATO forces were patrolling the East Coast of America. Could not an equally symbolic way have been found by the United States to harness NATO in the war against Afghanistan? This cavalier treatment of an organization purportedly at the heart of the American-European relationship certainly did not help matters as the Iraqi crisis unfolded; it seemed to me another reflection of the true state of the transatlantic alliance.

Paul Volcker

I met with Paul Volcker on a summer morning in his sunny corner office overlooking that icon of American capitalism–New York's Rockefeller Center. Volcker is one of the most prominent financial leaders of the last three decades. A towering figure physically as well as professionally, he served in the United States Federal Government for almost thirty years, under five presidents–both Republicans and Democrats. Crucially, for this book's purposes, he was chairman of the United States Federal Reserve Bank under Presidents Carter and Reagan during the 1970s and 1980s and witnessed firsthand the effects of the two major transatlantic rifts prior to the one over Iraq. He dealt extensively with European financial and political leaders in those years, and part of his very successful tenure as the Fed's chief was the ability to synthesize and interpret global developments and factor their meaning into action regarding American monetary policy. I wondered what his perspective might be on the nature of the current rift.

True to form, Volcker was characteristically blunt. "My sense is that from a political and security perspective this rift is worse, quite a lot worse," he told me. "We obviously had problems with putting missiles in Europe, pretty severe arguments, but I don't think it was a fundamental difficulty as we have at present." What accentuates this rift is that it is playing out against "the background development of a more self-conscious European commonality and the aggressiveness of a seemingly unilateral American policy."

Volcker, like Scowcroft and Clark, believes the French have always wanted to be the leaders in Europe. "They have always had the self-consciousness about their own grandeur and place in the world, and they thought here was an opportunity to assert that even more forcibly," he told me.

A European perspective adds yet another dimension to this book's unfolding picture of the transatlantic rift's complexity.

Ana Palacio

"The rifts we have seen are the tip of the iceberg that goes a long way down underneath," said Ana Palacio, who was Spain's minister of foreign affairs when we spoke. She served in the cabinet of Prime Minister Jose Maria Aznar, who, together with Prime Minister Blair of the United Kingdom, formed the nucleus of the European coalition that supported America's invasion of Iraq. A cabinet minister from a government that unequivocally supported the U.S. invasion of Iraq would bring valuable insight to the nature of this rift, I thought. And so she did.

"What is seen as a rift is really a series of rifts," she said, "not just across the Atlantic but within the European Union itself." According to Palacio, the threat of mutual destruction during the Cold War had kept the boiling cauldron covered and the rifts hidden; Iraq blew the lid off to reveal all the fault lines in the alliance.

Ana Palacio had served as Spain's minister of foreign affairs since July 2002. A lawyer by vocation, she was serving in her first senior government position when we met. She wants to give the impression that it is her sister–Loyola de Palacio, the well known EU Transport Commissioner–who is the real politician in the family. This self-effacing description, a sort of Spanish version of the American "I am just a poor country lawyer" routine, is quickly dispelled, as the European media and her fellow European foreign ministers had discovered as they watched Spain maneuver on the European political chessboard.

You may have started European integration, Palacio often reminded France and Germany when they threw their weight around, *but don't try to hijack the European Union—that belongs to all its members.* To make sure this position was driven home, Spain had joined with Poland in December 2003 to block ratification of the European constitution rather than give in to France and Germany, who insisted on changing the previously agreed balance of voting rights among the European Union's member states, to favor themselves.

Spain was also an enthusiastic supporter of the surprise letter in support of America's invasion of Iraq. Written on the eve of the Iraqi war by nine European countries, the totally unexpected development had thrown cold water on the French-German claim that *they* were the leaders of "European foreign policy" and that this "European" policy was implacably opposed to America's Iraqi invasion. The letter also made a dent in the French-German argument that European foreign policy was being consciously developed "by Europe" to serve as a counterweight to America's hegemony.

Palacio insisted the stakes for Europe in this rift were even greater than they at first appeared to be. While concurring with my American interlocutors that the rift is not ultimately about Iraq, and agreeing that the French-British competition for the leadership of Europe was an important contributor to the rift, she homed in on what to her was a much more important issue for Europeans: the future shape of the European Union and how its security will be maintained.

"Broadly speaking there are two security options for Europe," Palacio told me, "in NATO or outside NATO." Spain, along with many European states, is a strong proponent of a strengthened and expanded NATO as the ultimate guarantor of European security. "We Spaniards, with many others, oppose 'outside NATO,' we want to be in NATO," Palacio said. But there is another vision, according to her, which seeks an alternative, a counterweight or counterbalance to NATO that would cooperate with it but from the outside. A diplomatic reference to the French-German objective of developing the European Union's evolving common foreign and security policy as a counterbalance to what in France is termed America's *hyperpuissance*, or hyper-power status in the world. "That is what is at stake, and what we have been seeing these past weeks," she said, referring to the heated give and take during the lead-up to the Iraq war.

To Palacio the Cold War and its threat of mutual destruction also served as a soothing balm for the Europeans because it covered up all these internal conflicts, which are now surfacing as the rift over Iraq continues to play out.

The Iraqi war was by this time beginning to appear to be a sideshow rather than the major contributor to the European-American rift. It was becoming ever more evident to me that the growth of a

European "self-consciousness," as Volcker called it, triggered primarily by the ever growing integration of Europe, had generated tectonic shifts in the European political landscape.

There was now a new and an old Europe, though not in the sense in which American Defense Secretary Donald Rumsfeld had used the phrase to dismiss Germany's and France's opposition to a war with Iraq.[4] There was now a new and integrated European Union, as opposed to the old pre–EU Europe of separate and competing states that had fought each other for centuries. The European Union had transformed the quest for military leadership between European states into a tussle for political leadership instead. This emergence of a new European consciousness had its own dynamic. For leadership, the old Europe looked to America. The new Europe not only did not look to America for leadership but questioned it.

It is worth recalling that by far the majority of Europeans had opposed America's war against Iraq irrespective of their leaders' position. As we shall shortly see, the development of this new Europe over the past five decades had been largely ignored or pooh-poohed by American leaders. "American administrations have never understood the complexity of the European Union," former British Prime Minister John Major told me. The rift exposed by the Iraqi war went deep into the roots of the alliance's structure, but this was just becoming evident to most Americans and, I suspect, to many Europeans.

James Baker

A sense of quiet, understated power fills the Houston office of James A. Baker III. On a high floor of the Shell Oil building, an expansive office overlooks much of Houston through glass walls on three sides. It was a clear, early autumn morning in 2003 when we met there, and the view stretched to the Houston Ship Channel and the busy port of this southern American power center.

If your image of Houston is of one of those between-the-coasts cities that may matter in the oil business but not as an integral part of the geopolitical equation, you could not be more wrong. In addition to Baker, who was himself treasury secretary and secretary of state and continues to be a close Bush family troubleshooter, Houston is home to former President George H. W. Bush, and the two of them have helped establish local institutions that bring a continuous stream of world leaders to Houston. The former president's Library and Foundation are there, as is the James A. Baker III Institute at Rice University—a prolific foreign policy think tank run by the dynamic diplomat

Edward Djerejian, one of America's leading Middle-East experts, who has been United States Ambassador to Israel and Syria. The Houston branch of New York's Asia Society is an active and vibrant part of the Houston international scene, which now also includes a growing and thriving South Asian immigrant population.

Baker is part of the family that founded Houston, and that quiet, understated power results equally from his roots and from his own unquestioned accomplishments as a lawyer, diplomat, and public servant. Charm and graciousness and steel is how I would describe my first moments with Secretary Baker. Walk into his office and you get the unmistakable impression that if something really difficult had to get done, one would want to come to this room and try to convince its occupant to take charge.

Secretary Baker has played a significant role in helping shape recent European history and the path of modern European-American relations. He dealt with the European states when the European Union was still called the European Community and the process of European integration was trying to find its sea legs. He was part of the management team—together with Scowcroft and the elder Bush—that so successfully handled the unification of Germany and the aftermath of the Soviet Union's implosion. Under his watch the first chapters of the Balkans crisis unfolded, and he saw firsthand the problems Europeans had in formulating a policy to deal with this crisis in their own backyard. I had made the trek to Houston to make sure this book incorporated the opinion of this knowledgeable and still very active diplomat.

"I think this rift is deeper than the differences we have had before," Baker told me, "It is more generic and almost more personal." To Baker, the roles played by Germany and France during the lead-up to the Iraqi war were unacceptable and a point of departure from any previous behavior by these alliance partners.

To understand some of Baker's reasons for feeling the way he does, it is worth recalling that the United Kingdom, France, and the Soviet Union were at best lukewarm, but mostly opposed to the unification of what were then East and West Germany. The first Bush administration, with Baker as secretary of state, recognized the geopolitical dividends that would result from the unification of Germany. The benefits would also include significant economic and political benefits for Germany, a vitally important Western ally that was the driving force of the European economy. And there was a good chance that a unified Germany would push the already crumbling Soviet Union over the precipice.

When I met with Baker, the headlines were full of coverage of the election campaign in Germany, a campaign in which German Chancellor

Gerhard Schroeder had been capitalizing on the anti-American mood of the German electorate to shore up an electoral victory.

Germany would never have been unified, Baker reminded me, if the United States had not stood up and "pressured the British our close allies, we pressured the French, we pressured the Soviet Union, to take advantage of the window of opportunity and unify Germany," Baker told me. This took enormous political capital and strained long-standing relationships, but, as history has shown, it was what had to be done. So it was incomprehensible to Baker that ten years later a German chancellor could come to power on the back of America. "I mean, the leader of one of our closest European partners campaigning for power on an anti-American platform and *succeeding.*"[5] The hurt and anger were palpable in that room.

Then Baker fired the second barrel—at France, which had, in advance, threatened to veto the second Security Council Resolution on Iraq regardless of what the Resolution was. Again, it is worthwhile traveling back to the tumultuous early March 2003 days when the United States administration, against the wishes of its hard-liners, had decided to solicit approval from the Security Council for a second Iraqi resolution that could be interpreted as a UN authorization for war against Iraq. President Bush and Secretary of State Colin Powell worked the telephones to lobby the African and South American delegates who could provide America the majority vote in the nine-member Security Council. The bedrock nature of the alliance led the American side to assume that France, after expressing its considerable opposition to American policy on Iraq, would abstain in the final Security Council vote. But, it was at this juncture that France stunned many of the alliance partners, especially the United States, by announcing, in advance of seeing any text, that it would veto the resolution no matter how it was worded. "Now I have a lot of experience with the United Nations and that is outrageous behavior," Baker told me. It is impossible to describe here the contempt with which "outrageous" was uttered.

I was once told by a Washington publisher that George H. W. Bush became president because of his thoughtfulness in writing notes to each and every person he met. His skill at generating personal ties was illustrated by the fact that during the first Gulf War he had put together, using his personal contacts and the telephone, the unprecedented European-Arab-American coalition to evict Saddam Hussein from Kuwait. His son, now president, seemed not to have those skills.

So I asked Baker whether he and the elder Bush, if they had still been in office at this important crossroads for the alliance, indeed for the world, they wouldn't have picked up the telephone, dialed the

French President, and invited themselves over for breakfast to cut through the grandstanding that was going on? "Maybe so, but I am not so sure, as I told you it was more personal this time," Baker said.

But, and this is an important but, there is no question in Baker's mind that "we have an important stake in maintaining the transatlantic alliance." It is still important to America and Europe. There is to him an entire community of interests that are not debated or argued about between the Europeans and Americans—terrorism, trade, cultural things. "So even though it is a fundamentally deeper divide, we ought not to let our disappointments cloud our judgment," Baker warns.

It is a sentiment with which every interlocutor in this book would concur. But, as this chapter is beginning to reveal, and as the rest of this book will demonstrate, the geopolitical realities on which the alliance was based have changed, and it is not going to be as easy any more.

There were, however, two important dissenters to the idea that this rift is fundamentally different from past ones and will not be easy to repair: Senator Chuck Hagel of Nebraska and former British Prime Minister John Major.

Chuck Hagel and George H. W. Bush

Chuck Hagel is the ranking Republican on the Senate's Committee on Foreign Relations and is highly respected by his peers as one of very few senators who understands the historical sweep of American foreign policy and the importance of alliances in policy formulation. He takes a hands-on interest in foreign and security policy by meeting regularly with officials of other countries to buttress his own analysis, and he is supported by some of the best staff in the United States Senate. A respected Midwesterner from Nebraska, Hagel always says what he believes, and in all the years I have known him, he has never changed his mind just to be on the popular side of a political debate.

"You mentioned some of the past rifts, I'll mention a couple more," Hagel told me. "Vietnam for one, we had a major, major rift over Vietnam. Go back to the Fifties—Suez Canal was another. Suez was very interesting because we were on different sides from the British on that occasion." Hagel believes these transatlantic differences have always been there and will continue to be there, but the really important issue is how to resolve the differences without fracturing the relationship, and he is convinced Europe and America have been very successful at that in the past and will also repair this rift. "Some of our rifts were brutal, bitter and deep, but, because we have stayed focused on the common interests of all of our nations, we have been able to get through them, and I think we will continue to do that," he said.

The response of former President George H. W. Bush to my question on the nature of the rift seemed to be close to Senator Hagel's. But the former president pointed out that "the recent tensions are a continuation of differences that began with Charles De Gaulle and have surfaced from time to time." Bush wanted, it seemed to me, to draw my attention to the crossroads at which the European-American alliance had found itself in 1964, and the road President De Gaulle of France selected for France when he developed France's own nuclear deterrent and opted out of the unified American-led NATO force arrangement. By its decision, France began the long journey of severing the unquestioning leadership of Europe by America. The rift over Iraq simply uncovered a process that had become irreversible with the advent of what is now called the European Union.

It is a crossroads worth revisiting. At an important press conference,[6] De Gaulle began by acknowledging that, immediately after World War II, "For the countries of the free world, threatened by the Soviets' ambition, American leadership could then seem inevitable." De Gaulle described how America had continued to remain in charge of political and strategic policy for the Western alliance, projecting its influence either directly or through international organizations such as NATO that served as its channels to control the conduct of global policy. But De Gaulle went on to warn that, with such developments as the economic and military recovery of the western European countries, the appearances of weaknesses and divisions in the formerly monolithic Communist world, and the emergence of new states in the Third World, "the division of the world into two camps, led by Washington and Moscow respectively, corresponds less and less to the real situation." In an important observation, De Gaulle declared that the reasons why Europe had subordinated itself to America were "fading away day by day"–nearly forty years before the Iraqi war.

The elder Bush said, "Europe's foreign policy debates are a reminder that there are major issues that remain unresolved, including France's longstanding sensitivity to American influence in Europe, the changing role of a united Germany, and the effect of the European Union's new members." Ever an alliance optimist, he was quick to remind me that, "however those issues are resolved, America and Europe are always going to have differences, but among real friends . . . such as the United States and the European Union and its members, things have a habit of sorting themselves out."

John Major

The other dissenter, John Major, was British prime minister from 1990 to1997. Major and the elder Bush developed a close relationship during the first Gulf War that lasts to this day. Major is an unabashed admirer of the United States and the transatlantic alliance. He is now an international businessman, and I caught up with him on a snowy December 2003 morning at his elegant suite in a hotel on Manhattan's East Side.

Major has been a keen observer of both the alliance and the development of the European Union. He is also a fervent believer in the power of business to keep the alliance from disintegrating and refuses to believe the current rift is materially different from the other challenges faced by Europe and America.

The bombing of Libya in the 1980s? "A different problem," he told me. Many people took the view it was an excessive reaction, not a view Major shares. But "What one has to bear in mind is there are two European nations in particular that have a very close relationship with what, generically, you can call the Middle East. One is Britain, and the other is France. And that relationship is not only historical and political—it is economic as well," Major said.The siting of intermediate-range ballistic missiles (ICBMs) in the 1980s provoked great hostility, especially in Germany, which, after World War II, has had a wholly different identity, looks very warily at its twentieth-century past, "and has, as a result of that, the strongest, most powerful, and most virile peace movement anywhere in Europe," Major said. That was the core of the European opposition, he told me. Secondly, he continued, the Europeans felt that siting ICBMs in Europe "would increase Europe's vulnerability to a surprise attack from the Soviet Union. Those were the perfectly logical reasons for it, but things settled down and the rift went away."

Regarding the third dispute—over Iraq—Major maintains that France probably knows Iraq better than any other European nation. It has a much greater trading link with Iraq, and was keen to preserve its trading link as well as to reflect its historical relationship. "The French opposition to the regime change proposals in Iraq were based on two key components: their historical relationship with Iraq, and their frustration that this was not to be a United Nations operation. I think those were probably the two really big reasons for the French opposition," Major says.

As to whether the current rift is likely to prove to be a permanent rift, in Major's view, from the European perspective it will not. "The glue is not as strong as at the time of the Soviet Union, but it is still pretty strong, and the direct trading relationships between the countries supply, like a likely spider's web, an infinite number of links that are not broken," he said.

Serious Trouble for the Alliance

I wish I could be as optimistic about the current European-American rift as Hagel and Major, two leaders for whom I have the highest regard, but I am not. To me the alliance is in serious trouble, and here I fall in with the majority of my interlocutors.

The daunting set of issues and the downward spiral of the transatlantic relationship should be of real concern to Americans, for three main reasons.

First, as Europe continues to build the European Union, it is fast emerging as a potential rival to America's global supremacy. Do we want to disengage at this crucial time and not be able to influence the future shape and direction of the new Europe's policies? As former President Bush told me, "The Europeans are in the process of trying to forge a common understanding about security and foreign policy. It's important for the United States to participate in the dialogue from the beginning—which will ensure that America is treated as the ally that it is and not a competitor."

Second, Europe is the United States' most natural ally in the fight against terrorism. Both share a common idea of an individual's place in society and relationship to government; the concepts of democracy and liberty are woven into the fabric of the alliance. Facing an uncertain future scarred by the general availability of destructive technologies and a growing clash between competing visions of statehood, the alliance can substantially increase the odds that freedom will prevail.

America may have the most powerful military force in the world by far, but "there is a crying need not just to kill terrorists, but to try and figure out what kind of a phenomenon it is and how to deal with it at its roots," Scowcroft says. With the Europeans' far longer experience with terrorism, and deeper understanding of Islam and the East, the European-American partnership stands a far better chance of overcoming this gruesome chapter of world history than America attempting to face this threat alone.

Finally, as a recent report from Johns Hopkins University[7] shows, the transatlantic commercial relationship is the biggest and strongest in the world. More than half of the profits of American firms come from Europe; U.S. assets in Germany—$300 billion in 2000—were greater than total U.S. assets in all of South America; 13 million Americans and Europeans owe their livelihood to cross-investment between Europe and the United States; there is more European investment in Texas alone than all American investment in Japan.

Fortunately, so far the political rift between America and Europe has not damaged the commercial relationship–it can even be argued that the commercial relationship's vibrancy has kept the political rift from getting worse. But if the rift does get worse, it could cause real damage to American and European jobs and standards of living. How easily this can happen was demonstrated during the fall of 2003, when the European Union gave the United States three weeks to dismantle tariffs on steel imports or face $2.2 billion in retaliatory tariffs[8] on a host of American products carefully chosen to cause maximum political damage for an American president about to begin a re-election campaign. The United States backed down and removed the tariffs.

So, it is in both sides' interest to rebuild the alliance. But without realizing that this rift is fundamentally different, and coming to terms with the reasons why this is so, efforts to put the relationship back on track will be an exercise in frustration. As we shall soon see, in addition to such basic issues as the meaning of the phrase "war on terrorism" and the legality of how the United States has chosen to conduct its anti-terrorist operations, rebuilding the alliance faces an overarching obstacle.

As of the summer of 2006, the Republican Party controls both houses of Congress and, without a sea-change in the attitude of the American voter, will continue to do so for the immediate future. There is today a serious divide within the Republican Party's ranks with respect to the direction and conduct of American foreign policy. The traditional wing of the Republican Party, which believes the bond between Europe and America is critical and the alliance must be the cornerstone of American foreign policy, has been eclipsed in influence by the transformationalists and neoconservatives, who have no sympathy for long-term bonds and believe the challenges of the new century must be met by ad-hoc coalitions of the willing, put together as the need arises.

Although some of the neoconservative officials have left the present administration and moved on, their influence has taken deep root and continues to channel the conduct of present American foreign policy. Neoconservatives may not have pulled all the nails out of the European-American relationship, but they have certainly moved an already rocky alliance to its tipping point with their influence in managing the lead-up to the Iraq war and the invasion itself.

To deepen our understanding of the rift, we need now to look at the lessons both sides can take away from the Iraqi adventure.

CHAPTER TWO

Lessons from Iraq

We cannot function in this kind of a world in a unilateral fashion, coalitions of the willing are not by themselves the building blocks for a stable world.

—Chuck Hagel, United States Senator, Nebraska

In 1991, the Republican administration, faced with Iraq's brazen invasion of Kuwait, drew a line in the sand. American leadership and diplomacy created a groundbreaking global alliance that included Europe, America, and virtually the entire Arab world. This was no mean feat, considering that the war was directed against Iraq, an Arab country. Even the Soviet Union joined the alliance, despite of the fact that the Cold War was still active. Under a United Nations resolution—the only time the United Nations had unanimously authorized force against a member state—America led its allies into war and drove Iraq out of Kuwait. The powerful allied fighting machine could easily have moved on to Baghdad, but astute statesmanship and an ingrained respect for the United Nations, which had authorized only the recovery of Kuwait, required that the invasion stop. And stop it did. It was the high-water mark of American leadership since World War II and left its allies with a warm glow of accomplishment in a righteous cause.

In 2003, another Republican administration, against the wishes of its key European allies, with little Arab support, and in defiance of the wishes of the United Nations, invaded Iraq to overthrow the regime of Saddam Hussein. This time it was America's long-time European allies who drew a line in the sand, refusing to take part in the Iraqi war. For all practical purposes, in this second Gulf war America had one ally—the United Kingdom. This war was the low-water mark of American leadership and left most of America's traditional allies with feelings of anger and disillusionment.

The floor of the United Nations was the setting for the drama that preceded the American invasion. The United States had tried to use the imminent threat of Iraqi weapons of mass destruction as justification for its invasion and slugged it out with a disbelieving Security Council led by France and Germany. The world watched with fascination and bewilderment at the spectacle of these Western allies competing to court votes from countries that had thus far remained a cipher in global diplomacy but were now transformed into geopolitical heavyweights because of their occupation of the temporary Security Council seats.

As America's arguments for invading Iraq continued to lose backers, it announced that it would try one more time to get a resolution authorizing it to wage war against Iraq through the Security Council, but that it was prepared to take action irrespective of the wishes of the international community. France, in its own preemptive strike, declared it would veto any UN resolution to go to war without even looking at it. Germany and Russia joined the veto brigade.

The die was cast. America went off to war; the United Nations lay crippled and the transatlantic alliance seemed destined for the history books. Lost in this mess was the sad fact that no European leader supported Saddam Hussein or would have shed a tear at his eviction. Would that the allies had followed that old Arab saying: "My enemy's enemy is my friend."

The American administration repeatedly made the point that the Iraqi invasion was not unilateral because a number of countries took part in it. To charges that most of America's traditional allies opposed its attack on Iraq, the administration said that did not matter, the attacks of September 11 had changed everything. From now on, the war on terror would not be fought by America with its traditional allies, but instead by "coalitions of the willing." The fluid and dynamic nature of the terrorist threat meant America could no longer take the time to build a consensus for action with its traditional allies, and it did not need them to fight its wars anyway. America alone would decide on a course of action, and, once it had made this decision, it would ask for a show of hands and charge ahead with a coalition of whatever countries were willing to support its case, irrespective of their size or potential contribution to the war effort, and irrespective of whether they were democracies or dictatorships. Their moral support and willingness to be listed on the American side of the ledger were all that mattered.

Chuck Hagel's Prophecy

The American invasion of Iraq began to expose the decayed underpinnings of the European-American alliance, as we have seen in the last chapter. But the invasion of Iraq illuminated, in addition to the rift with America's major allies, a growing divide within Republican ranks. Important elements within the party disagreed, and continue to disagree, with the American administration's reason for going to war and its novel reformulation of the concept of alliances. Senator Chuck Hagel is one of them.

"Technically was our invasion of Iraq unilateral?" Senator Hagel asked rhetorically. "No, because the British were there, and there was a lot of conversation and chatter from other countries about supporting the United States; but the Brits were the only ones there with forces on the ground," he said. The main lesson from Iraq was clear for Hagel: "We cannot function in this kind of a world in a unilateral fashion," he told me. A few weeks later, quoting Joseph Nye, dean of the Kennedy School of Government at Harvard University, he said that "Crisis-driven 'coalitions of the willing' are not by themselves the building blocks for a stable world. We need to think more broadly and more strategically."[1]

Besides his senior position on the Senate's Foreign Relations Committee, Hagel is a decorated Vietnam veteran, an enormous supporter of the military and America's global responsibilities. His Nebraska roots reflect the conservative American Midwest and give his remarks special significance. One of his most important traits is that he takes principled, thought-out positions. Once he has taken them, he does not change, come what may (which is, in my opinion, a rare and diminishing commodity in politicians these days).

Hagel believes that whenever America acts unilaterally, it gets into trouble; he points to America's disastrous experience in Vietnam. "We had the support of the South Koreans, Thais, and Australians," he said, "but the rest of the world was opposed to what we were doing there, and that was a costly experience for this country."

Iraq too has been a costly experience for the United States, an experience that, in light of Vietnam, should have been avoided. Hagel was dead set against taking action without broad international support for the Iraqi war, and he believes the United States should have spent more time thinking through the Iraqi crisis: Who would govern when Saddam Hussein was gone? Who would pay to put all the pieces back together, as well as for the intended and unintended consequences that would surely follow, and are following? "We did not think that through very well, and those are also important lessons I hope we can learn," he told me.

Hagel is on particularly strong ground when he speaks about the costs of the Iraqi war for the United States, because he was one of few elected officials who personally tried to understand what the war would mean to America in terms of troops, money, and duration. The administration's expectation was that Iraq would be a relatively minor skirmish. The Iraqi army would be quickly defeated; the Iraqi people would welcome the conquering American troops; Iraqi oil would pay for rebuilding the country and for transforming it into a Western-style democracy. And, in a matter of months, most of the American troops would return home and leave Iraq to a grateful citizenry. Administration officials, however, had been hesitant to provide Congress with hard numbers or evidence to support these claims because the invasion was the result of neoconservative hubris, unsupported by Americans who had experience in the Arab world.

So Hagel, the ranking Republican on the Senate Committee on Foreign Relations, and Senator Joseph Biden, the ranking Democrat on the Committee, visited northern Iraq in early December 2002, as war loomed, to take a bipartisan measure of the situation and to try and find out what Iraq was likely to cost the American taxpayer. What they discovered in Iraq was poles apart from what the American people had been led to believe the war would be like.

In a *Washington Post* editorial dated December 20, 2002, titled "Iraq: The Decade After," Hagel and Biden wrote: "Once he (Saddam Hussein) is gone, expectations are high that coalition forces will remain in large numbers to stabilize Iraq and support a civic administration . . . as many as 75,000 troops may be necessary, at a cost of up to $20 billion a year . . . Americans are largely unprepared for such an undertaking . . . President Bush must make clear to the American people the scale of the commitment."

Would that the Iraqi story had followed the dismal Hagel-Biden script. Reality has proven far worse. Writing in the *Christian Science Monitor* on May 19, 2005, Peter Grier cited a new estimate by the Congressional Budget Office that said the costs for conducting the Iraqi war were running at $5 billion a month (three times the Hagel-Biden estimate) and by 2010 the war's costs could well total $600 billion. As of May 2006, as I write these words, there are still over 150,000 Americans in Iraq some four years after the invasion began. And after the death of more than 2,300 Americans and an estimated 50,000 to 100,000 Iraqis, there appears no light at the end of the tunnel. Not only has Iraqi oil not paid for this war—there isn't enough Iraqi oil being pumped for Iraqis to fill their cars' gas tanks.

Hagel had discussed Iraq with European leaders for months and says there was no European leader who needed to be convinced about the brutality of Saddam Hussein's regime; not one believed he could be rehabilitated. Given this transatlantic unanimity of opinion on Iraq, it should have been the perfect crisis around which to build an American-European consensus. But then it became a question of how and when to remove Hussein, and the strategy and tactics of "taking care" of him, and that is when it [the consensus] broke down. Another lesson that Hagel draws from this for both sides is, as he says, "We can work through issues if we are more patient and listen to each other's arguments and needs."

Given that nobody on either side of the Atlantic wanted to salvage Saddam Hussein, it must surely rank as one of America's major diplomatic failures that it was unable to cobble together an Iraqi policy with the Europeans prior to launching a war.

Clark, Baker, and Scowcroft on Going to War

Would a few more weeks' delay really have made a big difference to the success or failure of the enterprise?

There were three reasons why the American administration felt it could not afford to spend any more time in negotiation or consensus building. One was the treacherous Iraqi summer, when temperatures became unbearably hot for battle. To avoid fighting in these temperatures, the attack had to begin by the end of March 2002. The main reason, however, was the administration's opinion that there was an imminent threat to American security from Iraqi weapons of mass destruction. Neither argument sounded convincing to my interlocutors, and the "imminent-threat" argument has since been widely discredited.

The hot-Iraqi-summer argument is one that General Wesley Clark finds absurd: "as though the soldiers and their equipment would cease functioning once the Iraqi climate reached a specific temperature." He goes on to say that in 1990 the American deployments to Saudi Arabia were undertaken in temperatures that were routinely in the 130 degree Fahrenheit range without any degradation of the troops' fighting ability.[2] (My own conversations with senior field-grade United States Army officers have convinced me that a future enemy of the United States ought not to make military plans based on the assumption that American armor does not work in hot weather, unless that enemy wants to commit suicide.)

Clark's observations are particularly relevant because they are based on his thirty-seven year army career, which included the command of a run-down tank battalion whose tanks the previous commander had been unable to maintain. Clark was given six weeks to fix the maintenance problems and get the unit in battle-ready condition, and he did. Clark then ran the Army's National Training Center, and helped draft a report on the lessons from Army actions in the first Gulf War,[3] all of which make him especially qualified to speak about desert warfare.

But there were two reasons the United States did not wish to exert any more patience, or engage in further consultations with its European allies. The first was its argument (later proven to be totally fallacious) that there was an imminent threat to American security from Iraqi weapons of mass destruction. It was an argument that Hagel did not even bother to bring up and one of which James A. Baker III, Secretary of State under President George H.W. Bush, did not seem to think much of either. In addition to the weapons-of-mass-destruction argument, the administration forcefully trumpeted an alleged alliance between the Iraqi regime and al-Qaeda, a claim the administration made over the continued and forceful objections of the intelligence community. It too was later revealed to be untrue.

Secretary Baker had been part of the administration that had secured unanimous UN approval to use force to dislodge Iraq from Kuwait in 1991. Although the Cold War was still going on, the Soviet Union voted for the resolution authorizing use of force, even though Iraq had been one of its most important client states. In fact, this was the only time in its history that the United Nations was able to overcome the political difficulties of getting international approval for the use of force. It was by any measure a signal victory for American diplomacy. Why, besides the far more multilateral administration of the first Bush administration, had this happened? "We also had an egregious fact situation to deal with," Baker told me, referring to the spectacle of a big country invading and brutalizing its small neighbor. "We had something that was a little bit easier to sell than the idea of a war of choice to depose a regime."

What makes Baker's statement so ironic is this phrase—*war of choice*—which was at the heart of European criticism of the American invasion of Iraq. The vast majority of Europeans did not believe that facts on the ground supported the American position that Iraq constituted an imminent threat; they suspected that the real reason for the American action was simply the desire to oust Saddam Hussein—a suspicion that Baker's words appear to reinforce.

Baker's disagreement with America's policy on Iraq had already surfaced as early as the summer of 2002. Writing in a *New York Times* op-ed on August 25, 2002, Baker, while agreeing that military force might ultimately be needed to get rid of Hussein, had nevertheless advised the administration to not go it alone (as had Brent Scowcroft, the other key architect of the former Bush's foreign policy).

So, why would a Republican administration be so keen to start a war in the Middle East when such experienced Republican foreign policy experts as Hagel, Baker, and Scowcroft urged otherwise? The answer lies in today's bifurcated state of American foreign policy, caused by the divide within Republican ranks between the traditionalists and the transformationalists, who have starkly contrasting views about America's role in the world and the conduct of its foreign policy.

The traditionalists, who resided mainly in the State Department led by Colin Powell (until they were shown the door and Powell himself was replaced by Condoleezza Rice, a Powell competitor in the Bush administration), believe that "as America seeks to solve problems in the world it ought to work with its friends and allies within international organizations," Scowcroft told me.

The other group, the transformationalists, found largely in the Defense Department and the White House National Security Council, are inspired by neoconservative philosophy and believe the United States must use its predominant power to transform the world while it is in this unique position. In their view, "The place to start is the most benighted region of the world—the Middle East—where democracy is nowhere present, where the growth rates are abysmal and conflict is endemic," Scowcroft said. "And the starting point to bring democracy to the region is Iraq." It is the neoconservative vision that dominates United States policy today, and it does not bode well for the alliance's future prospects.

Brent Scowcroft, the National Security Advisor during the first Gulf War, was one of the key architects of the coalition that President George H. W. Bush put together to forcibly remove Iraq from Kuwait. A lifelong Republican, Scowcroft is widely considered to be one of America's most gifted and accomplished foreign policy experts. He was and is opposed to the American invasion of Iraq.

Scowcroft is clear that the main lesson for the United States from the Iraqi war is that, "while its close friends and allies the Europeans can be a pain in the neck, we are the custodians of a common philosophy—man and his relationship to the state and society—and that whatever pain there is in putting up and dealing with them, we pay a *heavy* price when they are not with us," he said.

These starkly opposing views of how America should act in the world is another reason the outcome of the present transatlantic rift will be fundamentally different from previous ones. It will be difficult if not impossible to rebuild the alliance if the neoconservative philosophy continues to influence America's foreign policy.

Division in the EU

Just as the Iraqi war shone a powerful light on the fault line within Republican ranks, it also illuminated a serious divide within the European Union. It turns out the harmonious united-Europe image the Europeans like to project may not be so harmonious after all. "A key lesson of the rift over the Iraqi war is that if anything has been hurt more than the transatlantic relationship, it is the European Union," argues Secretary Baker.

The European Union has been very successful in breaking down the barriers to trade within Europe and creating a huge business grouping and capital market. But the success in creating a single market has not yet translated into a single European foreign policy. That is not for want of trying, however. It must have been very heartening for France and Germany—who consider themselves to be the leaders of the European Union—to see the overwhelming majority of Europe's population support their opposition to the Iraqi war. They must also have seen this rallying of Europe's population as vindication of France's long-held conviction that the European Union should act as a geopolitical counterbalance to America. It was, they must have felt, the beginning of a "European" foreign policy.

And then, in mid-January 2003, out of the blue and with the Iraqi war only weeks away, nine EU countries co-signed a letter, published in the *Wall Street Journal* and several European papers, *in support* of the American position on Iraq. Many of these countries had just joined the European Union—Hungary, Poland, the Czech Republic, Slovakia—but there were also EU stalwarts such as Italy, Spain, Portugal, Denmark, and of course, the United Kingdom.

To the East European countries what the French, especially, were trying to do was anathema to them, because they view the presence of the United States in Europe as their security blanket. Their reasons for joining the European Union are largely economic, a business transaction; and although they may rely on their European partners for trade, for their security they want the United States. Even in the fifteen core EU countries there were splits, but its new members, particularly the Eastern Europeans, were *solidly* opposed to what the French were trying to do. Why? "To the extent Eastern Europe has a security problem, it is to their east [in Russia]. What is their solution to that? United States troops in Europe," Scowcroft explained.The letter was a clear shot across the bow of Germany, France, and the countries that agree with them that the European Union should, in time, become a geopolitical counterweight to the United States. In spite of the fact their populations overwhelmingly opposed the Iraqi war, the leaders of the countries that wrote the letter believed an open break with America would cause it to disengage from Europe, an action that, they believed, would weaken their security. They were not about to let that happen, even at the risk of undermining the already dubious claims of a "European Foreign Policy." The letter evoked an emotional outburst from France–whose President called the co-signers "badly brought up." But the cat was out of the bag.

Scowcroft's point reminded me of a dinner I had in the spring of 2003 with a senior East European official. He helped the head of his country make the decision to sign that famous letter. The official told me that his government's main concern was its relationship with the United States and only secondarily what the letter's impact might be on his country's relations with the European Union. Signing the letter would infuriate Brussels; not signing it would infuriate Washington. It was for them a no-brainer, and they signed the letter.

Writing in the *New York Times* on January 31, 2003, John Tagliabue summarized this European divide perfectly. The Iraqi debate, he wrote, "is generating not an Iraqi problem but a European problem, a growing split between nations like France and Germany that are defending a narrower, European interest and those looking to a broader, North Atlantic alliance."

To many American observers the divide within the European Union was a clear lesson in the futility of the Europeans' attempts to devise a common European foreign policy, a key plank of what was to be the new European Constitution. It was being debated in 2004 when I began to write this book, but it was unceremoniously rejected in 2005. The American Defense Secretary, only half tongue-in-cheek, had pronounced Europe divided into "new Europe" and "old Europe." So much, it would seem, for Europe's plans to balance the United States on the global stage.

Ana Palacio on the Real Strength of the European Union

But does this European divide really mean that the European Union's strategic objective of moving from a purely commercial entity to a political union is impractical, and the creation of a "European" foreign policy just wishful thinking?

It is a conclusion that Ana de Palacio, Spain's erstwhile foreign minister, cautions is wrong and misleading. Without minimizing the importance of the European divide, she believes the real lesson that should be taken away from the shooting down of the European Constitutional Treaty is that the strenuous differences over it are *a result of the success already achieved by the European Union.* In time, "because of the Iraqi crisis," Palacio told me, "the European Constitution will be much more ambitious than it might otherwise have been in dealing with foreign policy."

What she means is that, up to this point, the Europeans had been preoccupied with the structural issues of creating a single market: dismantling borders and tariffs, introducing a single currency, and rationalizing business laws. The Iraqi war forced Europe to operate at a whole different level in the continuing process of constructing the European Union, as illustrated by their even considering a common European foreign policy. The American push to wage a pre-emptive war on Iraq, a sovereign state, for reasons in which the overwhelming majority of Europeans did not believe, forced the Europeans, for the first time, to confront a real issue of foreign policy—both as citizens of their own countries and also as Europeans.

"In siding with American action against Iraq," Palacio explained, she is defending a policy she would like to see "not just as a Spanish minister, but also as a European." And it is her hope that in time there will be a European forum to discuss a unified policy and a channel to convey the resulting consensus to the outside world.

Palacio is not unduly concerned about the rift, because she recognizes it as being a consequence of *"la nature des choses"* [the nature of things]. The fact of the matter is "We now have leaped forward to address a real issue of foreign policy." Iraq transformed theoretical discussions on whether and how to construct a "European" foreign policy into a concrete debate: whether to support the Western alliance's leader of fifty years—the United States—in its war against Iraq, or not. "And, this has brought the member states' differing perspectives to the surface for the first time."

Europe was publicly forced to confront its own perspectives on foreign policy and to face up to its divisions. Palacio is not surprised by the resulting rift and does not believe it will prove fatal to the European Union's objective of developing a common foreign policy. I find myself in her camp, based on my experience (more on this subject in a later chapter) of trying to change a then popularly held American opinion that the Europeans would never have a common currency. They did, and the euro is now the second most powerful currency in the world after the U.S. dollar.

But even a year before the euro's launch, most Americans had not even heard of it, and many of those who had simply could not believe that Europeans would give up one of the most cherished symbols of a country's sovereignty—its currency. (BBC Television covered a conference that the Foreign Policy Association and my then company Niche Systems had organized on the business impact of the euro. One nattily dressed American executive they interviewed thought the euro was a new European airline!) If there is anything the growth of the European Union teaches us, it is that the Europeans are determined to create an ever closer union, come what may, and that the United States ignores this at its own peril. I therefore believe they will do the same in constructing a common European foreign policy, which is an important reason to rebuild the European-American alliance. As former President Bush stated, it would be far better to be their partner now then when their foreign policy has coalesced.

Even as the political environment in America is not conducive to rebuilding the alliance, the European states are coalescing into an ever closer and tighter entity. What is worse is that the very issue that now dominates American foreign policy—the all encompassing "war on terrorism" doctrine—has itself become a divisive issue for the alliance.

Hugo Paemen on the War on Terrorism

The events of September 11, 2001, were felt in Europe just as strongly as they were in the United States. The sense of solidarity that Europeans felt was palpable and was captured in the headline of an editorial in the French daily newspaper *Le Monde* on September 12, 2001. "We are all Americans," wrote its editor Jean-Marie Colombani. "In this tragic moment, when words seem so inadequate to express the shock people feel, the first thing that comes to mind is this: We are all Americans!" he pronounced.

Once the United States established the connection between Al-Qaida and the terrorism inflicted on New York and Washington, Europeans were in complete support of the need to attack Al-Qaida's home base of Afghanistan. The war backed by the United Nations and led by the United States, to root out the terrorist camps and destroy Al-Qaida's leadership, had wide support in Europe. As the attacks against terrorist targets in Afghanistan changed to talk of a global war on terrorism, to a clash between the forces of good and evil, however, Europeans and Americans stopped seeing eye-to-eye.

Europeans opposed the Iraqi invasion by overwhelming majorities, even in countries whose governments chose to side with the United States. Over 90 percent of Spaniards, 87 percent of Italians, and 79 percent of Poles were against the American action. Even in the United Kingdom, America's closest ally, over 55 percent of the population was opposed to the war, and, in an even more stunning finding, fully 57 percent of Britons agreed with the statement that American foreign policy contributed to the September 11 attacks.[4]

Hugo Paemen, the former EU ambassador to the United States, believes that it is important for both sides to try and understand the differing American and European perspectives on the terrorist strikes of September 11.

Europeans have a long experience of continued terrorist threats on their own continent: the Baader-Meinhof gang in Germany, the Red Brigades in Italy, the Irish Republican Army (IRA) in the United Kingdom, and the Basque revolutionary group Euskadi Ta Askatasuna (ETA) in Spain. It is worth recalling that in the three decades before the Madrid train bombings on March 11, 2004, hundreds of Spaniards had been killed by ETA terrorists. According to Amnesty International the group deliberately targeted civilians, political representatives, and government councilors.[5] In one particularly gruesome act, fifteen shoppers, including women and children, died in 1987 when an ETA bomb had exploded in a Barcelona supermarket. The IRA terrorists spread random death and destruction throughout Northern Ireland and also in Great Britain. Prime Minister Margaret Thatcher herself barely survived an assassination attempt in 1984.

The terrorism tragically inflicted in Madrid on March 11, 2004, when terrorists bombed a crowded commuter train, shows up another example of the difference in European and American reactions to a terrorist act. Spain's population is about a fifth of America's. Without taking anything away from the horrific brutality of September 11, the effect of seeing almost two hundred of their countrymen killed in Madrid must have been as terrible for Spain as the three thousand killed in New York was for the United States. Yet the rule of law was not suspended, and there appears to be complete transparency in the arrests and detention of suspects, and no general "war" was declared or Guantanamo-like detention facilities set up.

The twenty-five countries of the European Union, meeting on March 21, 2004, barely two weeks after the terrorist attacks in Madrid, appointed a terrorism czar to coordinate the European anti-terrorism efforts. They made it clear, however, that Europe's heightened efforts to combat terrorism would not dilute their democratic institutions and free societies. "Europe is not at war," Javier Solana, the European Union's foreign policy czar, told Germany's *Bild am Sonntag* newspaper. "We must oppose terrorism energetically, but we must not change our way of life. We are democrats who love freedom."[6]

"So although the Europeans were equally horrified by what had happened on 9/11, the events were differently perceived there," Hugo Paemen, the EU Ambassador to the United States, says. The phenomenon of irregular organizations out to kill innocent civilians to create a reign of terror for what they consider to be a higher ideal—convinced that they cannot reach their goal through the normal channels—is a notion Europeans were already familiar with, even if they were shocked by the extent of the September 11 tragedy.

The United States, on the other hand, had never experienced this kind of sustained aggression within its borders and had never felt so utterly vulnerable. There had been the Unabomber and Timothy McVeigh relatively recently, but these constituted individual, isolated cases, and therefore the perception and thus their impact were less extreme.

Although September 11 initially united Europeans and Americans in their feelings of shock and horror, "the rumblings [from America] of an on-going, no-end-in-sight global war that followed shunned European public opinion away," Paemen said. After the attack on Iraq, the disconnect between them was complete. "Are We Still 'American'?" asked *Le Monde's* Colombani in a *Wall Street Journal* editorial on March 9, 2004. This time, in contrast to two and a half years earlier, he wasn't so sure.

As another gauge of the divide between European and American perceptions, it is important to understand what the word "war" itself signifies on either side of the Atlantic.

For the majority of the Americans, Paemen explained, war is a kind of heroic event. Courageous young men go to a faraway land to fight for what they consider to be the good cause, with all the technology and moral support the nation can muster and determined to show the rest of the world what they are capable of. They return victorious, they are celebrated; even the families of those who were killed are proud that these men and women sacrificed their lives for the nation.

"But for most Europeans war is synonymous with seeing your own city destroyed and a lot of innocent victims, often your own family, killed. It is not a heroic event at all," he said. The American action represented the threat of a war and all its horrors without a clearly defined target, "shifting from Osama bin Laden to Al-Qaida to Iraq, and possibly to other countries. It made the Europeans somewhat suspicious as the perception grew that there was no clear American agenda," Paemen said.

It helps to know Paemen a bit to fully appreciate his remarks. Were Central Casting asked to pick someone to play the soft-spoken, urbane, and intellectual European diplomat, they would certainly have Hugo Paemen on their short list. Paemen was the ambassador of the European Union to the United States from 1995 to 1999. It was on his watch that the euro was launched, and it fell to Paemen to convince a largely skeptical and seemingly uninterested American public that eleven European countries would give up their currencies and adopt the euro; that the euro was just not another anti-American idea cooked up to fight the dollar, as the newspapers seemed to think; and that it would ultimately be good for America.

From 1987 to1995 he worked as deputy director general for external relations for the European Commission (the European Union's civil service) and successfully led the European negotiation team during the World Trade Organization-Uruguay Trade Round. He understands the bargaining power of a European-American partnership in global negotiations as very few people do. Paemen was instrumental in helping strike working compromises in difficult transatlantic disagreements on issues such as genetic foods labeling and computer data privacy.

At this time I had also become involved in explaining the impact of the euro and European monetary union on American business strategy and public policy, so our paths had crossed a number of times. I was aware of Paemen's sensitivity to both American and European attitudes and felt his views would sharpen the opinions I was getting for this book. We met in his Washington, D.C., law office; he also maintains one in Brussels and appears to be in constant motion between the two.

Paemen is a thoughtful, erudite, lifelong diplomat, a strong supporter of the United States and the alliance, so his blunt statements seem doubly effective. He now added yet another dimension to the unfolding picture of the differing European-American perspectives on September 11 and its aftermath.

"If the Europeans were uneasy with the war on terrorism concept, the related quasi-religious 'good against evil' view taken by the United States made them even more uneasy," Paemen said. Perhaps because of their longer history, the Europeans have known for some time now that God is not always on their side. "Witness the endless religious wars in Europe during which Catholics murdered Protestants and Protestants murdered Catholics." In Europe's more recent history the Third Reich tried to use the slogan "*Gott mit uns*" [God is with us] to legitimize death and destruction. In fact, even today's suicide bombers act out of religious conviction. "So, the notion that you are always on the right side and that God is with you makes most Europeans very, very, uneasy," Paemen explained.

Lessons to Take Away from Iraq

Ana Palacio

The overarching lesson from the Iraqi crisis for both sides, Palacio believes, is the recognition that the existing transatlantic relationship needs to be adapted to fit today's world. "We have a relationship that is based on an old concept—the Cold War, which does not exist any more," she told me. "The Iraq issue has surfaced the fact that this relationship has not adapted to the new circumstances." There is an urgent need for dialogue to accomplish this, and the very first item she would place on the agenda is the meaning of the phrase "war against terrorism," because it means something very different on either side of the Atlantic. I was struck by the similarity of Palacio's and Paemen's observations.

During the Cold War, the Soviet nuclear threat had been met by the Western alliance's strategy of mutually assured destruction. Europe and America, in one voice, told the Soviet Union that if it chose to fight a nuclear war, the alliance would incinerate it, as it was getting inciner- ated. No one would win. The strategy and its execution had the unequiv- ocal endorsement of Europeans and Americans.

There is no such agreement about America's war on terrorism, nei- ther of the phrase, nor of its method of execution as adopted by the United States. For Europeans, the fight against terrorism has been fought for years and continues to be fought with the "penal code in one hand, and laws and procedures in the other," Palacio said. In contrast, America has reacted to September 11 by declaring a war and fighting it, without any penal code and outside the rule of law according to the European perspective. This has resulted in situations such as Guantanamo, where the United States has imprisoned hundreds of people without charges, trials, or access to lawyers, on an offshore base (on otherwise hostile Cuba) so as not to be subject to its own domestic jurisprudence. "Guan- tanamo was a major error on the part of the United States," Palacio told me with obvious sadness because of her government's support of the war in Iraq. America is based on the rule of law, she says, it is very respectful of human rights. "How can you just declare this to be a war that is to be fought without any of these principles?" she asked.

This illustrates what Palacio means when she said the alliance needs to be updated in view of the new threats. The differing perceptions of the American war on terrorism is an issue she feels needs urgent discussion.

Since September 11, the entire thrust of America's foreign policy seems to be contained in the phrase "war on terrorism." Nothing else appears to matter. Yet here is the foreign minister of one of America's strongest European allies who does not believe this phrase even means the same thing in Europe, and who is openly critical of the civil-liberty depriving actions the United States undertakes under the overarching mantle of its war on terrorism. Genuine sympathy for the murdered 9/11 victims does not mean automatic European acceptance of the American war on terrorism.

Palacio also has a tough message for her fellow Europeans. Europe must understand that while its legalistic approach is appropriate when dealing with an interlocutor who is on the same level legally, if one is dealing with a failed or rogue-state, unless there is a real threat of the use of force, "You are stuck, you cannot deliver." And here she brings up a very European obstacle. For European society generally–as evidenced by the antiwar protests in London, Paris, and Berlin–the use of force is very difficult to come to terms with, and this attitude is deeply embedded in the psychology of Europe. "America does not suffer the guilt of a colonial past, of having set in motion wars all over the world," she says.

Hugo Paemen

I asked Paemen about the European side. What lessons do they take away? He paused a moment then focused his remarks entirely on France's aggressive opposition to the Iraqi invasion in the United Nations, especially its threat to veto an as yet unseen resolution to the Security Council.

"I hope the French have learnt from the rift that they cannot play with European decision making," he told me. "And just as the American side lost credit with world opinion, France's actions damaged the credibility of European institutions in the eyes of Europe's public opinion."

The European Union has been built treaty by treaty, consensus by consensus, in unanimous decisions laboriously arrived at by the member states, a shaky decision-making process that has never generated much enthusiasm among average Europeans. Paemen has no doubt this process was further weakened by France's actions. With so many important decisions pending to continue moving European integration forward, he wonders whether the damage done will now prevent the process from reaching a satisfactory ending.

"So, for us in Europe, the lesson to be learnt from all this is that we should be more careful in the future, particularly when it concerns the relations with our only strong ally, and first talk to each other," he said.

John Major

Paemen's sentiment was echoed by John Major, the former British prime minister, who had a pointed, one-sentence lesson he would like the United States to take away: "Consult first, act later."

Major brings another unique perspective to the alliance. His father had dual citizenship: American and British. Major himself travels to America often and is very much connected with Europe, so he has both perspectives. He served the United Kingdom for seven years as prime minister, from 1990 to 1997. Before that he had won acclaim for his work as Prime Minister Margaret Thatcher's Foreign Secretary and Chancellor of the Exchequer (the equivalent of America's Treasury Secretary).

I caught up with Major on a brisk morning in New York as he was wrapping up his latest American visit. His is a reasoned, balanced, even professorial voice. The answers are concise and–refreshingly for a politician–unequivocal.

As for the European side, he thinks the key lesson they should take away is that the French pushed the opposition too far by indicating they would veto a UN resolution. "I think that was unwise, it damaged the United Nations and brought forward the day when the United Nation's Security Council will be reformed by changing its present composition which is untenable," he says.

Wesley Clark

Reflecting on his NATO military experience, Wesley Clark said the other key lesson the United States needs to take away is that in Iraq it did not apply the lessons learned during the Kosovo war, and got into trouble. "There is nothing wrong with military power," he believes, but one has to use it for the appropriate purpose. "What we learned by waging modern war in Kosovo[7] was that if you line up and take advantage of international law and diplomacy, you can achieve strategically decisive results without using decisive force." He believes the Bush administration failed to understand that lesson in either Afghanistan or Iraq, and now there is hell to pay with the consequences in Iraq.

Clark also told me the United States needs to ask itself why it believes the Middle East, not Southeast Asia, not Northeast Asia, not South Asia, is the one area in the world where America feels it can use force almost with impunity. "People there don't like to be forced to do things, any more than people anywhere else like to be forced to do things. If we lived in a country where people parachuted in wearing strange outfits, covering up their faces and causing problems with the families and destroying our industries, we might shoot them. They might be from Mars or some place," he said.

I wanted to know whether, being the pre-eminent power in the world, we should be proactive in changing the world in our image–the city on the hill, so to speak.

"I do subscribe to it," Clark says, "I believe in a new American century, but I believe in using the methods that we used in Europe. If we had tried to take over Europe in the same way we tried to take over Iraq, we could have had the Third World War there towards the end. Now I am not saying the Middle East is as easy a nut to crack, it's far more difficult, culturally, religiously and historically. But we have always viewed it as somehow an area in which it was appropriate to use force, that it wouldn't respond to these other influences, aren't we a victim of our own hubris in that case?" he asked.

These fractures between the United States and Europe show why it will be difficult for the alliance to just come back together again. They also begin to shed light on the new reality to which a reconstituted alliance will have to conform.

What about the North Atlantic Treaty Organization (NATO)? Surely, while we have NATO, the alliance can never fall apart? Well, to use George Gershwin's lyric, "it ain't necessarily so."

CHAPTER THREE

NATO: Corpse on a Horse?

A lot of people have made their whole careers out of NATO and are dedicated to preserving it.

—Paul Volcker

Most Europeans and Americans would be hard pressed to tell the difference between the phrases "Atlantic alliance" and the "North Atlantic Treaty Organization" (NATO), so closely intertwined are they in the day-to-day vernacular of the relationship. In fact, for many Europeans and Americans NATO *is* the alliance.

NATO is the security arm of the North Atlantic Treaty, which was set up in 1949 to connect the United States permanently to the defense of Europe against Soviet-Communist domination. NATO met this threat with flying colors and helped maintain the peace with its powerful American-led multination deterrent capabilities for fifty-four years, until the collapse of the Soviet Union in the early 1990s. So effective was the deterrent symbolized by the NATO forces that the Cold War was won without the need for NATO to fire a single shot. Today the Cold War is history, as is the Soviet Union. Erstwhile members of the Warsaw Pact—NATO's nemesis during the Cold War—are now themselves proud new NATO members.

NATO was always conceived as much more than a military alliance. Dean Acheson, then United States secretary of state and one of NATO's key architects, said the treaty "sought to add the power of the United States to create a true balance of power in Europe as a stabilizing and preventive force. The treaty was more than a purely military treaty. It was a means and a vehicle for closer political, economic and security cooperation with Western Europe."

So, can there really be a major divide between Europe and America when that powerful entity, NATO, still exists?

Unfortunately, as we are about to see, the answer to that question is yes. Not only does the divide exist in spite of NATO, but the attempt to remake NATO as a global fighting machine makes the divide worse. NATO has become a source of continuing friction in the European-American relationship because it has no agreed mission any more and because it is being forced to take on a new mission—operating anywhere in the world—for which it is singularly unqualified.

There is also the long-forgotten close connection between NATO and the United Nations—an organization not held in great esteem by many Americans, but considered by Europeans and much of the rest of the world to be the basis of international law. The United Nations was barely two years old when NATO was created, and the designers of the Treaty went out of their way to ensure that the United Nations' umbrella of legitimacy covered their newly minted Western alliance. Witness the opening sentence of the Treaty's Preamble: "The Parties to this Treaty reaffirm their faith in the purposes and principles of the *Charter of the United Nations* (emphasis in the treaty) and their desire to live in peace with all peoples and all governments."[1]

The drafters and signatory countries were careful to thread the United Nations, especially its Security Council, into the fabric of the Treaty, as Article 7 demonstrates: "This treaty does not affect, and shall not be interpreted as affecting in any way, . . . the primary responsibility of the Security Council for the maintenance of international peace and security."

Try to reconcile Article 7 with the post–September 11 American appointment of itself as the guardian of world peace and security or with the American invasion of Iraq, which was carried out in blatant disregard of the Security Council, and the reason for NATO's irrelevance today comes into focus. Without a consensus to use force among the United States, the European Union, and the United Nations, NATO cannot be used. And the United States has stepped away from operating in this collaborative fashion because the guiding principle for American policy today is: you are with us, or you are against us, but you have no say in what we decide. This policy is fundamentally at odds with NATO's.

"Your point about the closeness of NATO and the United Nations is a very good one, because we have lost, if we ever understood, the connection between those two organizations," Senator Chuck Hagel told me. A different perspective was offered by a former high-level official, who chose to remain anonymous, who is a master practitioner of the art of political hardball. When I pointed out the close linkage between NATO and the United Nations, he told me with a wry smile, "Nobody pays any attention to it; that is just not the way things operate."

To be sure, NATO has in the past been used to bypass the role of the Security Council. "We did all the Balkans stuff through NATO because we knew the Russians would veto it [in the Security-Council]," the same former high-level official told me. These workarounds were feasible as long as it was possible to take the time to develop a European-American consensus on the objective for which NATO was to be used. This consensual world was terminated by the United States after September 11, however, and without a return to collaborative decision making with the Europeans, it will be impossible to use NATO in this way again.

The United States had ceased to worry about the link between NATO and the United Nations as America prepared for the Iraqi invasion, when the Europeans resurrected it. Turkey, a NATO member, asked the organization to supply it with defensive weaponry in advance of the impending American invasion in case of a retaliatory attack by Iraq.

In spite of strong support for Turkey's request from the United States, NATO's leader, three NATO members–Belgium, France, and Germany– blocked the Turkish request for arms to protect itself. "Outrageous" is how this was termed by American officials and analysts; it was nothing short of letting down a NATO member, they said. But, as a French official told the *New York Times* on February 11, 2003, "Our position is coherent, if we are not yet deciding to go to war in the Security Council, we cannot decide to go to war at NATO. Once the Security Council authorizes force against Iraq, it will be very easy to send material to Turkey right away."[2]

The link between NATO and the United Nations is part of a world order that the Western powers created after the Second World War, and to use NATO without consideration of its ties to the United Nations would release a series of aftershocks with unpredictable consequences.

Hagel continues to be a a strong supporter of NATO. "It is relevant, it does have a purpose, and without NATO you start to loosen a process that in my opinion, and I think in the opinion of a lot of people, has helped keep peace in the world for fifty-eight years," he told me. Hagel views it as one of the group of indispensable institutions that were put together after World War II by far-thinking statesmen to preserve global security and underpin the world's economy. One of the reasons Hagel has been so effective on the Senate's Foreign Relations Committee is his detailed understanding of these global organizations and the complex web of interconnections that link them together. It is a system still crucial, he believes, to maintaining an ordered world.

"We need to keep reminding ourselves why the United Nations was born. And NATO, and all these multilateral institutions–The World Bank, IMF, GATT and so on–that Bretton Woods[3] produced," he told me. "They were produced as forums and organizations to deal with the common threats and common interests of countries. You cannot have NATO without the United Nations, you can't have some of these pieces without the other pieces, because all of it was part of a plan," he says.

"These multilateral institutions were inter-linked building blocks designed by some of America's pre-eminent thinkers and statesmen– Cordell Hull, George Marshall, Dean Acheson, President[s] Truman and Eisenhower being some of them," Hagel explained. "They and many others who worked on these issues deserve real credit for what they achieved, and it is really important to understand their accomplishments," he said. "They just didn't say, 'let's do a little NATO work over here and invent something there, and then maybe we will do a little United Nations and we will kind of come up with a better League of Nations part two.' No, it all fit."

In Hagel's opinion we need NATO and the United Nations more than we ever have. "There are reasons for those organizations," he told me, "and there will be more and more reasons developed in the future as to why they are important."

Hagel is right on the mark with his observations. A part of the answer to the question of whether there can really be a divide between Europe and America while NATO still exists lies in facing the reality that NATO functioned when Europeans and Americans played by the same rules of global engagement. There was broad agreement between them on who the common enemy was and when and how military force could be used. These rules of engagement–at the heart of NATO–were demolished when the United States chose to act pre-emptively by invading Iraq without Security Council authorization and in the face of opposition from leading European countries. Under America's new rules of engagement America, all by itself, could decide who the enemy was, declare war, and attack unilaterally anywhere in the world. The rest of the world simply had to accept America's verdict. "You are with us, or you are on the side of terrorism," President Bush had declared. France, Germany, and Russia had begged to disagree and blocked any participation in the Iraqi war by NATO. If NATO cannot be deployed in the "global war on terror" (except on the margins, as it is in Afghanistan)–a war on which, the United States maintains, the existence of the civilized world depends–can NATO really be relevant any more? Without consensus between the Europeans and Americans on how force is to be used, isn't NATO today more like a corpse on a horse, rather than the powerful knight in shining armor it is still presumed and portrayed to be?

NATO's impotence was again on display in April 2004. The United States had by then already become bogged down in Iraq in a guerrilla war (on its way to becoming a communal-civil war) and increasingly found itself without the necessary military manpower to confront the deteriorating situation. To overcome this shortage and to put an international face on the Iraqi war, United States Secretary of State Colin Powell, urged NATO to become involved in Iraq by sending European troops under its auspices. In an almost immediate rebuff for the United States–NATO's supposed leader–both France and Germany challenged Powell's decision to ask NATO for help without first getting UN approval, and the Secretary's request was stillborn.

The Europeans had again served notice that for NATO to be invoked as a mutual security alliance, the United States had to play by the established rules. These rules placed the Security Council at the center of the world order and required its approval before force could be used against a sovereign state.

Absent this stamp of approval by the United Nations, the United States was on its own, they said. America continued to maintain that it did not need permission from the United Nations to defend itself, a position that the majority of Europeans opposed, viewing the Iraqi war as a unilateral American invasion, not an act of self-defense. Between the lines, and not so subtly, the Europeans were transmitting another, more profound, message: *You may have been the unquestioned leader of NATO in the years after World War II, but you are not today. If you want to use NATO you need to convince us of your cause and build a European-American consensus. Otherwise, you are on your own.*

As important an issue as the UN link poses, NATO has a much more fundamental problem: with the demise of the Soviet Union, the main reason for its existence has disappeared. It does not have a mission any more, and is scrounging around to find one.

"NATO was built on a military alliance against Russia, which doesn't seem to make much sense any more," Paul Volcker told me. "A lot of people have made their whole careers out of NATO and are dedicated to preserving it. I think it would be better if we found some kind of a substitute for it because some kind of a political alliance is a good idea. But I don't know how you find a substitute for it without then to begin thinking about what to do about the United Nations, and that becomes impossible."

NATO's supporters believe the organization is still relevant, and they want it to survive by using NATO beyond the area implied by its name, the North Atlantic–to give it an "out of area" or "out of theater" role in officialspeak. But actions speak louder than words. Bypassed in the attack on Afghanistan, irrelevant to the Iraqi war, NATO is clawing out a marginal post-war support, stabilization, and reconstruction role in Afghanistan.

By this role in Afghanistan (a role approved by the Security Council, meaning America had to build consensus for it with the Europeans), NATO wants to demonstrate that it is still relevant, that it does not have to be a Europe-centric organization, that it can be called on to fight anywhere in the world. The strategy is central, NATO believes, to its survival because there is little if any need for its services in Europe–the European Union's military forces are taking over the conflicts in its backyard, such as Kosovo and Macedonia, and there is no Soviet Union to fight against any more. So the success of NATO's deployment in Afghanistan may well be its do or die moment. But, if this is the case, NATO might as well fold its tent and leave the world stage.

In May 2004, months after NATO moved into Afghanistan, its military commanders were bitterly complaining that military support promised its Afghanistan contingent six months previously had yet to be delivered. For instance, on paper NATO has access to over a thousand helicopters, which are the military workhorses in this land of inhospitable mountainous terrain. Yet not even the grand total of four promised at the beginning of 2004 had shown up. Lack of personnel and equipment were forcing NATO to restrict its operations to just one city– Afghanistan's capital, Kabul. It could not even think about its stabilization mission, which required it to provide security in outlying areas of Afghanistan to ensure the success of elections. Besides personnel, NATO was short of aircraft, communications and logistical equipment, firepower, and high-technology weaponry.[4] Rather than leading the charge, NATO was hanging on by its fingernails. Reporting in *The Financial Times* on May 19, 2004, Judy Dempsey reported that Jaap de Hoop Scheffer, NATO's Secretary-General, had told ambassadors of NATO member countries at their regular NATO meeting in Brussels that "Member states must immediately deliver the personnel and equipment they had promised." NATO's peacekeeping mission in Afghanistan was at a critical juncture and could fail, Scheffer warned. So much for NATO's attempt to demonstrate its "out-of-area" capabilities.

Reflecting in December 2005 on the *BBC News* Web site, the veteran newsman Rashid Khalid pointed out that even in their peacekeeping role, each NATO country's forces have a list of just what they will do and not do–national caveats, as they are called. For instance, "Spanish troops based in the West [of Afghanistan] will rarely leave their compound; German troops in the North will allow no other NATO troops to fly in their helicopters."[5]

"Insurgents Emboldened by Plan for NATO Forces to Replace the U.S." was the headline of a column written by Carlotta Gall in the May

3, 2006, issue of the *New York Times*. Reporting about the worsening situation in Southern Afghanistan, Gall wrote that news of the American troop pullout in the coming months and their "handing matters over to NATO peacekeepers, who have repeatedly stated that they are not going to fight terrorists, has given a lift to the insurgents, and increased the fears of Afghans."

Besides the lack of equipment and the absence of cohesiveness, there is the almost comic process used by NATO to make battle decisions. NATO makes decisions by seeking consensus among its members. Building consensus was relatively simple when all of its members faced the possibility of nuclear incineration from the massively equipped forces of the Soviet Union. Once this nuclear threat ended, consensus-building among NATO became a wholly different matter, as the only war that NATO has ever fought–in Kosovo–demonstrated. Every enemy target had to be approved by consensus. Here is Wesley Clark's description of NATO's decision-making mechanism: "the foreign ministries, or in the American case, the State Department, ran the day-to-day process at NATO headquarters through nations' ambassadors, who met in the North Atlantic Council or NAC. The defense ministries were represented within the ambassadors' teams and also by a military representative of the Chief of Defense who sat on the NATO Military Committee, a body subordinate to the NAC. Thus the foreign ministries had the upper hand and the last word in working the issues."[6] In plain English, two committees had to reach consensus separately to bomb a target, with each member of each committee watching out for political fallout from his superior.

Is it any wonder that the U.S. troops in Afghanistan that are involved in tracking down al-Qaeda and Taliban remnants will not come under NATO's command, and that when NATO graciously offered its services after September 11 to help launch the initial attack against Afghanistan, the United States was not even remotely interested? "We would never let anyone tell us who we can and can't bomb again," Secretary of Defense Rumsfeld reputedly told Wesley Clark after 9/11, referring to the manner in which NATO's only war was fought.

To further complicate the issue, consider the role of France–the largest and most potent military force in Europe, with the possible exception of the United Kingdom. France withdrew from NATO altogether in 1966 after developing its own nuclear force, and in protest against American domination of the organization. In 1993 it rejoined the NAC but refused to join NATO's Military Committee. Under this bifurcated membership arrangement, France could approve a NATO military operation yet not commit any forces to it, thereby depriving NATO of the military assets of its largest member (after the United States)! This

French arrangement led to the following exquisite comment with the same former high-level official quoted earlier when I asked him for suggestions to improve NATO: "One thing we ought to do is to tell France to get in or get out," he told me. "I'd say, 'Look, you want to have it both ways, you don't want to be in the military part of NATO, and yet you want to have a vote on what is done or not done with the military, well sorry, that old dog will no longer hunt.'"

NATO's decision-making process, which requires unanimity, was difficult enough when it comprised only the United States, Canada, and Western European countries. The process grew exponentially more difficult when the alliance expanded to include Eastern European countries. (As this book goes to press, there is even talk of including Australia and New Zealand.) Beyond the difficulties of making decisions, these new members changed the nature of the organization, further diluting its historic razor-sharp mission of defense against the Soviet Union, a mission that was already obsolete.

Brent Scowcroft was against NATO's expansion because to him, after the end of the Cold War, the issue was more what NATO was than what it did. "It is the membership of the United States in the security of Europe, and NATO was that visible commitment," he said. The world has changed, Scowcroft admits, and to survive, NATO must adjust to the new geopolitical realities. With its expansion, "I wonder whether NATO has the flexibility to adjust?" he asked.

As mentioned earlier, Paemen was a key negotiator during the World Trade Organization's Uruguay Round of trade negotiations. Thinking through a problem to its roots and using staff to sort out the unknowns before making a decision come as second nature to him. He is convinced that once the original idea of NATO—a strong defense against Soviet expansion—was no longer a realistic hypothesis, NATO's future role should have been thought through. "We should have tried to work out how would the roles be divided between a European Union which is becoming more and more something like a United States of Europe, not *the* United States of Europe but something like it, and how the two would work together," he said. "But don't forget that all these developments happened in a short period of time, and we were not prepared for them, so we haven't thought it through even today."Ambassador Hugo Paemen is not very comfortable with NATO's expansion either. While it may have been a good idea to expand NATO with countries from Eastern Europe that had belonged to the Soviet camp but now wanted to join NATO, "The expansion has also set up a contradiction," he said. "It is no longer the original NATO, and we have not found a credible profile for the new NATO in the international community. So this uncritical enlargement of NATO, while it may have been politically expedient, has undermined NATO's original concept."

Paemen's view takes on special meaning in light of the European plan to to set up a Rapid Deployment Force (RDF) of sixty thousand troops. A high-level EU planning staff (separate from NATO's planning mechanism) is already in place, and the fighting force itself is slowly but surely taking shape. Like every project that European states have undertaken in the interest of forging an integrated Europe, from the Coal and Steel Community to the euro, the RDF moves in fits and starts. Yet the Europeans are determined to have a defense capability within the European Union, and the smart betting is that it will happen, given that the European military-economic heavyweights—France, Germany, and the United Kingdom—are in favor of it.

"They have tried to extend NATO's reach into the political and economic area," Paul Volcker told me. But he is skeptical it can hold together without the previous common threat of annihilation by the Soviet Union. "You would have to convert it into something which has an interest in places other than Europe and defense against Russia, which is happening piecemeal, but I don't know if those interests are strong enough to hold NATO together," he said.

Finally, the war and occupation of Iraq, the American prison in Guantanamo, the persistent news stories about secret prisons around the world that hold Muslims, the breakdown of Muslim integration in Europe, and numerous other perceived and real slights have made the United States a pariah among the Islamic countries around the world. An attempt to strengthen NATO would now be perceived as another Western attempt to encircle Muslim lands.

All the North Atlantic Treaty ministers met in Washington on April 2, 1949, to sign the draft of the North Atlantic Treaty. The signing ceremony was dignified and colorful, with the President and Vice President of the United States in attendance. The U.S. Marine Band added a note of unexpected realism as the dignitaries waited for the ceremony to begin by playing two songs from the then currently popular musical play *Porgy and Bess*. They led off with "I've Got Plenty of Nothin'" and followed that up with "It Ain't Necessarily So."[7] It would appear that, fifty years later, NATO has finally begun to live up to those expectations.

But it *ain't* necessarily so. NATO's continuing difficulties result from now being asked to do a job for which it is unqualified. There is, as we shall see later, an important new mission that NATO could undertake, a mission for which it is uniquely qualified—a mission that is suited to the organization's proven accomplishments and to the challenges of the twenty-first century, if Europe and America (especially America) have the vision to see this.

CHAPTER FOUR

But They Won't Fight!

Nations will act when they believe there is a threat.

—Former United States President George H. W. Bush

> It is time to stop pretending that Europeans and Americans share a common view of the world, or even that they occupy the same world. On the all important question of power—the efficacy of power, the morality of power, the desirability of power—Americans and European perspectives are diverging . . . Europe is turning away from power . . . on major strategic and international questions today, Americans are from Mars and Europeans from Venus.

So Richard Kagan famously declared in his book *Of Paradise and Power*.[1] Published on the eve of the Iraqi war, it made headlines from Beijing to Paris. Many Europeans were outraged at what they considered a gross and inaccurate simplification of their feelings, while many Americans were pleased that at long last someone had dared to speak about the real reasons why the transatlantic alliance is simply not practical any longer: The Europeans are wimps.

With his creative twist on the phrase "men are from Mars and women are from Venus," Kagan created a provocative metaphor to describe the now-popular but totally inaccurate opinion in the United States about today's state of European strategic and security thinking, which goes something like this:

1. The Europeans have become soft and flabby and are now pretty useless when it comes to dealing with a world full of ruthless terrorists.

2. They don't want to fight to defend themselves; they would much rather talk and negotiate. And why shouldn't they, because

3. The United States has paid to garrison hundreds of thousands of troops in Europe to protect the Europeans. Thanks to American largesse, Europe has been able to defend itself with a first rate military without paying for it. The money this has saved has gone into developing Europe's cradle-to-grave social safety nets. And finally,

4. The very process of creating the European Union required European states to become inward looking. They had to spend all their time negotiating with each other as they gave up slices of their sovereignty to create the European Union, and having seen the successful result of their negotiations in Europe, they now believe all external disputes ought to be resolved by negotiations and not by war.

This last point bears repeating because it is in many ways the heart of the "Europeans are genetically soft" argument. In the process of developing the European Union, the Europeans, it seems, have changed. As they have given up sovereignty to establish their supranational union and worked through endless negotiations to create what has proven to be the first war-free Europe in centuries, they no longer believe in using force globally and in the expenditures that are required to create and maintain a potent military.

The creation of the European Union has been such an all-encompassing task, this thesis goes, that the Europeans simply don't have the time or the desire to face up to the growing threat of international terrorism. Even worse, success of European integration has misled Europe to believe that this European experience can be extrapolated to deal with terrorism. If centuries of enmity and hate in Europe can be overcome by a series of treaties, shouldn't all the world's ills be resolved in the same way? Of what possible use is such an ally in the hard and dangerous world of the twenty-first century?

This picture of the modern European state, so attractively packaged by Kagan, has obvious negative implications for rebuilding the transatlantic alliance and for the formulation of American foreign policy towards Europe. Is this really a true representation of the European state of mind?

"I don't believe it," Brent Scowcroft told me. "But I think if Europe felt threatened in one way or another, you would find a change in their defense spending. And for us to rail against Europe, it won't work and will make things worse," he said. Scowcroft believes the European defense budgets are decreasing because Europe does not see a threat of the civilization-destroying magnitude that America does.

"And that is where I think Kagan is dead *wrong*"—he leaned over and looked me directly in the eye as he delivered this word—"that Europe wears a petticoat—it is simply not true. Where the Europeans find their interest involved, they are probably more warlike than most other societies," Scowcroft said.

Criticism of the European approach to security usually begins with France and its disdain for projecting military power beyond its borders. The French are held up as the poster child for what is wrong with the European approach to the twenty-first century's security issues.

In reality, nothing could be further from the truth. In addition to a battle-ready force and the ability to wield nuclear power through a modern air force, France deploys troops in Kosovo, Bosnia-Herzegovina, and in the Ivory Coast and elsewhere in Africa. Thousands of French Special Forces comb the Afghan countryside with their American counterparts looking for Osama bin Laden and hunting for the Taliban. The French Navy patrols the Gulf of Aden and Oman.

"They have some of the finest intelligence in the world," Senator Chuck Hagel told me. "There is no question of their capability or willingness to fight if they have to. But it is like everything else, it is the priorities. How do you get there? Can you do it a different way? Can you accomplish what you need to accomplish without invading Iraq?"

The French also do not pull any punches when their security interests are at risk, especially in former French colonies. Chad is a landlocked African country and a former French colony that, among other things, pipes about 170,000 barrels of oil a day through Cameroon to the Atlantic Coast. About 1500 French nationals live in Chad, and France has been militarily involved there since 1986, when France intervened to prevent a Libyan seizure of Chadian territory and to keep a France-friendly Chadian government in power.[2] As of 2006, the French army had 1250 soldiers in the country. On April 14, 2006, Agence France Presse reported:

> A Chadian rebel leader has alleged that French fighter planes have bombed several rebel-held towns in eastern Chad, causing an unknown number of civilian casualties. France's defence ministry said a French Mirage jet had fired warning shots near a rebel column advancing on the capital N'Djamena from the east on Wednesday morning, as a "political signal" . . . with the framework of the security of our nationals in Chad.

Britain, of course, is in a class of its own when it comes to wars. "We have been at war almost every generation for a thousand years," Major told me. "We don't like wars, but the British are not particularly perturbed about wars," he added. As for France, he reminded me that the French intervened in the Bosnia and Kosovo crisis long before America arrived.

Wesley Clark was a Rhodes Scholar and takes his history very seriously. He scoffs at Kagan's thesis that the Europeans have been transformed into treaty-loving peaceniks as a result of their success in negotiating treaty after treaty to create today's twenty-five-nation European Union. He pointed out that Europeans had been witness to the power of negotiations against a supposedly unshakable ideology—Soviet Communism—that had shut off all of Eastern Europe.

"Kagan's analysis is elliptical," Clark told me. "The real origin of this thought [that treaties and negotiations can change the situation on the ground, as dangerous as it might be] is not the European Union but the Conference for Security and Cooperation in Europe (CSCE) treaty of 1975, in which Americans and Europeans joined together with the Soviet Union to end Second World War lock-in boundaries and to guarantee human rights in Eastern Europe."

In his famous 1946 speech at Westminster College in Fulton, Missouri, Winston Churchill memorably described the enslavement of Eastern European countries by the Soviet Union.

> From Stettin in the Baltic to Trieste in the Adriatic an iron curtain has descended across the Continent. Behind that line lie all the capitals of the ancient states of Central and Eastern Europe. Warsaw, Berlin, Prague, Vienna, Budapest, Belgrade, Bucharest and Sofia; all these famous cities and the populations around them in what I must call the Soviet sphere, and all are subject, in one form or another, not only to Soviet influence but to a very high and in some cases increasing measure of control from Moscow.[3]

Marshaling its allies, the United States formed an iron ring of military force around the Soviet Union and its satellite states. Western Europe became the front line against Soviet expansion. For years the Europeans had to live with the terrifying threat that comes from living in between a rock and a hard place: in this case, between enslavement and nuclear Armageddon.

Military containment of the Soviet Union stopped Communist expansion, but it was not until the CSCE treaty had been successfully negotiated in 1975 that a modicum of the old freedoms was restored to the countries that had been occupied.[4]

What brought about this change on the part of the Soviets? Two years of painstaking, at times frustrating, negotiations with the Soviet Union under the auspices of the Conference for Security and Cooperation in Europe.

The CSCE negotiations were conducted from 1973 to 1975, and the final landmark treaty was signed on August 1, 1975, in Helsinki, Finland, by the leaders of all the European countries, Canada, United States, and the Soviet Union. The Helsinki Accords, as the treaty was called, promised a major step forward for freedom in the Soviet satellite states in Eastern Europe; it embodied détente and presaged the process that ended the Cold War.

"At the time all of the Cold War realists, hard liners, and the military, guys like me, scoffed and asked: 'What can you do with treaties, words on a piece of paper?' Clark said. "Yet those treaties, a Polish Pope, a lot of support from the international labor movement, along with Afghanistan, brought down Soviet power and freed Eastern Europe." Those were important treaties, and their success in transforming Europe through continuous, tough negotiations are the real force behind European foreign policy, Clark believes.

So, to Clark the statement that the European preference for treaties and negotiations comes only from their experience in building the European Union is simply not true. "What they saw from the CSCE's results was a different method of warfare, a different method of protecting security. It was to use the strengths of the Western democracies rather than rely on old concepts," Clark told me. "The strengths of our democracies are to reach out, to embrace and to entangle and then to draw close, and that's what we did in Eastern Europe."

Europe and the United States pierced the Iron Curtain with economic reform in Hungary, with labor connections in Poland, and with tourism and travel in Czechoslovakia. "Citibank was as important as NATO in bringing down the Soviet Union and in persuading Hungary that it had to reform its corrupt and inefficient state industries if it was going to remain solvent," Clark said. "Eastern European countries were drawn in by tourism and trade, by Germans and Frenchmen, by the cultural connections and television and radio broadcasts from the West, by the exchange of students, and by multiple sets of ideas that, bit by bit, caused Europe to unify. After all you don't change people's mind by killing them, and we do the relationship a disservice by constantly harping on the military inequality," Clark concluded.

The Europeans have watched their entire continent get transformed by the power of negotiations, albeit backed by the steel of American power. They are witness to the results: For the first time in its recorded history Europe has been without war for fifty years. Is it any wonder that treaties and negotiations are at the heart of the European mindset? Can a new European-American alliance be crafted without accounting for this deep-seated European conviction in the efficiency of what Clark calls modern war?

That Kagan's Mars and Venus metaphor for the attitudes of the United States and Europe generated so many headlines is itself indicative of the nature of the divide between the erstwhile allies. Not one of the leaders I spoke to had anything but disdain for Kagan's thesis.

"Many disagreements of security issues can be explained by different European and American perceptions of the threats we face in the post-Cold War, post-September 11 world," former President Bush told me. No one needs to remind this decorated World War II veteran of the viciousness of Europeans on the battlefield. "Nations will act when they believe there is a threat," he said, "That is one reason why differences in European and American threat perceptions are so important." Prior to launching its Iraqi invasion, America was simply unable or unwilling to convince Europeans that their perspectives about the importance of Iraq in promoting terrorism were wrong. It was a failure of that basic building block of alliances—trust. To make colorful comparisons to Mars and Venus does a disservice to the years of diplomacy that created a multifaceted alliance that lasted throughout the twentieth century.

Former President Bush's good friend John Major was even more emphatic. "I don't think America understands the complexities of Europe, and I don't think Europe understands the psychology of the United States," he said. That, according to Major, leads to genuine misunderstandings of the motives of the two power blocs.

Perceptions, or rather misperceptions, are also central to Ana Palacio's analysis of the European-American relationship. When I asked her about Kagan's Mars/Venus analogy, she smiled and told me that the Europeans have a different way of explaining what they consider are the real differences between the two sides: "'Americans have the brute force, but we have the legitimacy,' which in the end is the same thing," she told me. "These are misperceptions and we have to overcome them. They are both equally wrong."

So strongly does she believe that both sides are prisoners of their perceptions that when I asked her whether it would have made any difference to the European support of the American invasion of Iraq had the European Union's 60,000-person Rapid Reaction Force been in place, her reply was an emphatic "No."

Politicians are quite effective in using perceptions for political advantage. The presumed docile nature of the Europeans is no exception to this rule. Senator Chuck Hagel put it succinctly when he told me that the processes Europeans and Americans follow in arriving at political decisions are a little different, and that sometimes drives a wedge between the two, and then "We begin ascribing insincere motives to each other and before you know it, we have a problem." It is important for leaders to stay above that, he said. I pressed my point with this savvy internationalist. Aren't the Europeans so changed that they don't look at the world as a dangerous place as we do, are no longer interested in using their military around the globe to fight terrorism, and are consequently untrustworthy allies? "I think there are some of us who have been far too harsh on our European friends," he told me. "Some in Congress and in this administration have assigned unsavory motives to some of our European partners." Politicians are particularly guilty, Hagel said, of inventing motives, and "then we assign those motives to opponents. We are both guilty of that, Europeans do it as well, and both of us have a responsibility to make the relationship work."

The impression that has been created in America that the Europeans are no longer interested in using their military power, with the result that their usefulness to a United States "at war" is questionable at best and a hindrance at worst is just flat wrong. Unfortunately, this inaccurate impression has further aggravated the divide.

Europeans do not view the world through the "war-on-terrorism" glasses as the United Stated does. They do not feel as threatened, and this is reflected in their military budgets. But the gap in military spending between the United States and the European Union is also due to the fact that European integration has not developed enough to produce a European defense policy, and the expenditures are still done on the basis of individual countries. To some extent, the Europeans *have* become used to having their defense underwritten by the American taxpayer throughout the Cold War.

When it comes to using force, the Europeans don't need lessons from anyone, but their preference is for first trying to resolve political disputes through multilateral organizations, especially the United Nations. Also, the Europeans simply don't agree with the post–September 11 neoconservative-inspired idea adopted by the American administration of transforming the world by force; they want a UN-centered world, not one centered on the United States.

It is a measure of the depth of the feelings between Europe and America that, four years after the invasion of Iraq, transatlantic tempers have not cooled. Not one European state besides the United Kingdom has stepped forward to help the United States by providing strong military or financial assistance in its Iraqi adventure. On the contrary, even states that were only a token part of the alliance are walking away, while America is faced with increasing carnage and hostility and a looming quagmire all on its own.

It did not have to be this way. America had to work hard to change the "We are all Americans" feeling of the overwhelming majority of Europeans after the attacks of September 11. A mighty alliance could have been formed with the European Union and the rest of the world to try to eradicate permanently the kind of terrorism that has now been loosed on the world.

But it was not to be. Europe was simply not that important for the go-it-alone, America-knows-best, our-way-or-no-way crowd that had picked up the reins of power in the United States. The result of this administration's foreign policy has been devastating. There was a time, not too long ago, when people around the world might have thought American foreign policy to be clumsy and bumbling, but they believed America's motives were pure. Most of the world does not believe that any more and the myth of the "ugly-American" has, in the space of a few years, been transformed into reality.

The real damage to America's relationship with Europe had begun years before, however, by America's neglect of, and dismissal of Europe's transformation into the European Union. Instead of locking arms with this new Europe, American politicians had chosen instead to rely on the so called "special relationship" with Britain. This was a serious mistake, and, as we are about to see, the preference for Britain has cost the United States dearly.

CHAPTER FIVE

The European Union: A Missed American Opportunity

I am not sure American administrations have understood the sheer complexity of the European Union.

— *John Major, former British Prime Minister*

In today's charged atmosphere of distrust between Europe and America, it is rarely remembered that the European Union owes its existence as much to American statesmanship as it does to European (especially French and German) vision and leadership. This makes it even more distressing that American foreign policy is now so out of line with European public opinion.

If there is to be any chance of rebuilding the trust that used to exist between the two, it is important to take the time to place today's transatlantic divide into a historical context. Let's wind back the clock to the sunny days after the end of the Second World War—specifically, to a fateful weekend in 1950 that marks the beginning of the European Union.

Sunday, May 7, 1950, turned out to be a bright, sunny spring morning in Paris as the U.S. Secretary of State's airplane touched down at Orly airport. On hand to greet Secretary Dean Acheson was the American ambassador to France, David Bruce. Acheson looked forward to a few restful days in Paris before he headed to London for yet another act in the quest to secure the postwar peace in Europe, an interminable political exercise that had controlled his days since the end of the Second World War.[1]

The days of the Allied occupation of Germany were drawing to a close. France and Germany were again becoming the industrial engines of continental Europe, and Germany's steel exports were already set to exceed France's. The question of how to integrate the resurgent German industrial giant peacefully into Europe was a central and vexing foreign policy issue for the allies.

The end of World War II had left America, with its monopoly of nuclear weapons, as the undisputed master of the universe, but that was then. The political horizon was very different this May morning: The Soviets had already tested an atomic bomb, ending America's monopoly of these most powerful weapons on earth; China had finally been conquered by Mao Zedong, thereby ensuring Communist control of this teeming country and signaling a global Communist partnership, bent on world domination. While these developments were taking place, the American defense budget had been reduced, and its powerful wartime armed forces disbanded. Acheson worried about the Allied position in Western Europe.

Important voices in America were calling for an integrated Europe, with the power and industrial vitality of Germany permanently anchored through France to Europe's growth and prosperity. It seemed to be the only way to ensure Europe's and ultimately America's future in what was once again viewed as an increasingly dangerous world.

How to do that? Europe had been ravaged by war for centuries. Its nation-states formed shifting power blocs that attempted to balance each other through an endless game of power politics and wars that had killed millions of Europeans. In this deadly game Germany and France had played a starring role,[2] and the bad blood between the countries was legendary. So, after World War II—the bloodiest conflict of them all—the idea of remaking Europe into a peaceful entity, with France and Germany at its center, must have seemed an impossible task, and was part of the problem that weighed on Acheson's mind that morning.

Unknown to Acheson, help was at hand from an unexpected quarter, in the person of Jean Monnet, a visionary French businessman. Monnet had also served as France's postwar economic commissioner, and the unity of Europe had become an obsession with him. Monnet was an accomplished transatlantic deal maker who appreciated the pragmatic Anglo-American way of doing things.

Monnet recognized that the old idea of uniting Europe politically under one grand design would never work; centuries of European enmity had put that idea to rest. To him, the secret to a united Europe lay in achieving the integration in small steps. The success of each step would create increasing amounts of European solidarity and move the

European states along the path of an ever-closer union. Monnet was also shrewd enough to realize that European integration required the elimination of centuries of enmity and distrust between France and Germany, continental Europe's dominant industrial powers. Industrial power at that time meant dominance in coal and steel, two necessary ingredients for waging war and the key to economic growth.

Monnet came up with the concept of uniting Europe by creating pools that he called communities of national resources and markets. For starters, he proposed the revolutionary idea of combining the coal and steel production of France and Germany and turning it over to a new supranational organization called the European Coal and Steel Community. The Coal and Steel Community would not be a cartel that would divide up the markets and assign quotas for companies. Instead, its goal was to eliminate the barriers to competition among states and encourage production to meet the rapidly growing demands of a resurgent Europe as it recovered from the devastation of World War II. It would also make it easier for the Allied powers to lift their controls over the amount of steel Germany was permitted to produce after the war, because the new European coal and steel entity would bind Germany and France within a broader economic community.

Monnet found a kindred spirit in France's foreign minister, Robert Schuman. The two quickly concluded that the secret to successfully launching the European integration plan was to get the Americans on board. Acheson's fateful arrival in Paris provided them with the opportunity to do this.

Instead of the respite he sought that weekend, Acheson wound up putting the American imprimatur on Monnet's grand political vision for Europe. This vision would ultimately convert Europe to a huge new economic-political entity with a geographic size, population, and economy to rival that of the United States. This was the week that the European Union was launched.

Upon landing, Acheson was surprised to hear from Ambassador Bruce that the French foreign minister, Schuman, intended to call on him that very day, a Sunday! Also, Schuman wished the meeting to be confidential, restricted to Schuman, Bruce, Acheson, and an interpreter. The visit proceeded as follows:

> No sooner were amenities observed than Schuman expounded the essentials of Monnet's idea that the whole French-German production of coal and steel be placed under a joint high authority, with the organization open to other European nations—what would later become known as the "Schuman Plan." It was, as Acheson wrote later, "So breathtaking a step toward the unification of Europe that at first I did not grasp it."

Schuman implored the two Americans not to speak of his plan to any of their colleagues until he had discussed the proposal with members of the French cabinet and, if they agreed, to then make a public statement in the National Assembly. Schuman said he was consulting Acheson because he believed that the scheme was wholly in accord with American policy, and he needed strong support from Washington to help his government push the plan through.

Acheson was especially impressed by the simple approach that Schuman brought to a big idea, "A far cry from that of American-trained trial lawyers." It was, as Bruce called it in a cable later that week, "The most imaginative and far-reaching approach that has been made for generations to the settlement of fundamental differences between France and Germany."[3]

Bruce and Acheson met with Monnet the next day and were completely sold. Acheson called the White House, shared Monnet's plan with President Truman, and asked him to support it when Schuman made the plan public. Truman concurred, and put America's imprimatur on what would arguably become one of the most important political developments of our time.

One year later, in Paris, on April 18, 1951, Germany, Belgium, Italy, Luxembourg, and the Netherlands accepted the French proposal and signed a treaty to give up domestic control of coal and steel production to a new organization called the European Coal and Steel Community.

I would like to highlight two important points with respect to this treaty. For the first time, six European countries had given up their sovereign powers over two vital commodities for the common European good. Also worth noting, Britain chose not to be a party to this momentous development. Both these points, especially Britain's decision to step away from Europe, were to have important consequences for Europe's future and, in turn, for the future of the transatlantic alliance.

The European Coal and Steel Community succeeded even beyond its founders' dreams. Within five years, coal and steel trade within the six countries had increased by over 129 percent.[4]

Within six years, the success of the Coal and Steel Community, together with the continued economic resurgence of Western Europe, led the six pioneering countries to sign additional treaties and yield even more sovereignty to two new communities. Meeting in Rome on March 25, 1957, the six established the European Economic Community (EEC) and the European Atomic Energy Community (EURATOM). The former replaced six separate national markets to create a single European market for the free movement of people, goods, services, and capital. EURATOM ended national control of atomic energy in the six members of the EEC and shifted it to a pan-European organization.

Over the next three decades European integration continued to broaden and deepen its structure. In 1965, for instance, the staff and institutions of the three communities were merged into one. By 1968, a customs union was completed, eighteen months ahead of schedule. Denmark, Ireland, and Britain (finally) joined the Community in 1973, and by 1979 the European Monetary System (EMS) became operational. It was based on a currency unit called the European Currency Unit or ECU, a measurement that reflected the value of all the currencies then represented in the Community. The ECU was an important way-station to a common European currency. By 1986, Greece, Spain, and Portugal had become members of the EEC.

In 1993, yet another treaty was signed in Maastricht in the Netherlands. It expanded the European Economic Community to move it towards a European Economic and Monetary Union, which momentously led to a new European single currency–the euro. In parallel with these developments, by 1995, the European Union (as the rapidly integrating Europe was now officially called) had expanded to Austria and Finland, for a total of fifteen countries in all. At the signing of each new treaty, EU member states gave up yet more of their sovereignty for the common European good. In the case of the euro, twelve of the fifteen countries gave up their currencies, together with their powers to set monetary policy.

Ten more countries (Poland, the Czech Republic, Hungary, Slovakia, Lithuania, Latvia, Slovenia, Estonia, Cyprus, and Malta) joined the European Union in May 2004; three more (Romania, Bulgaria, and Turkey) are scheduled to enter the European Union by 2014.

Today's twenty-five-member European Union has a GDP of around 10 trillion dollars, which matches that of America; and, a population of almost 500 million, which is greater than the populations of the United States, Canada, Japan, Australia, and New Zealand *combined*. It has a flag, an anthem, a high court with jurisdiction throughout Europe, a parliament, and an executive called the European Commission. Mechanisms are being designed to craft a European security and foreign policy under a European foreign minister and to deploy a European Union–flagged army of sixty thousand within sixty days, and keep it in the field for a year. Clearly, a major political-economic power has begun to take its place in the world alongside the United States and, although they are not a subject of this book, alongside China, India, and Russia.

In an increasing array of critical business areas including aviation, data privacy, satellite positioning technology, genetically modified food, the environment, and mergers and acquisitions, the United States now faces one European interlocutor, who brings to the table pre-agreed European policy and the clout to hammer out an agreement for all member states.

For instance, in 2001 the European Union's antitrust commissioner, Mario Monti, forbade the merger of two American companies, General Electric and Honeywell, even though American antitrust authorities had approved the merger. The American companies' substantial European businesses made them subject to European Union rules, a fact that General Electric seemed to have overlooked, or rather, in my opinion, have felt it could bypass with American government support.

To be sure, the European Union is not yet a United States of Europe, and European countries still jealously guard important parts of their remaining sovereignty over fiscal policy, defense, and security. But the direction appears quite clear—an economic entity of immense weight and growing political cohesiveness has taken shape and is not going away.

The speed, momentum, and success of the integration project has been breathtaking. For instance, while it took the United States over a hundred years and multiple attempts to organize its currency under the auspices of a central bank, it took the Europeans less than half that time to set up a European Union and launch its central bank and the euro. The ad hoc process of nibbling away at the fragmented states of Europe, however—as opposed to coming up with a blueprint for what the European Union would ultimately look like and then executing this plan—has created uncertainty, especially in the United States, about the ultimate objective of the integration. The uncertainty was exacerbated by the discordant notes that pinged out from the different parts of the European Union: it is first and foremost an economic bloc, it is really a political union, it is destined to become a geopolitical counterweight to the United States, and so on. "If Americans did not know quite where this process was going, the interesting thing is the Europeans themselves did not know it either," Hugo Paemen, the former EU Ambassador to the United States, said.

What the Europeans did know is that they had to terminate the chapter of their history in which European countries had fought one another at regular bloody intervals, and they have done this by following the pragmatic Monet-Schuman plan of gradual integration through shared Communities. "The essential characteristic of the European Union is that it is an agreement by European states to build up a legal order to which Europeans are surrendering important parts of our sovereignty," Ana Palacio, Spain's erstwhile Foreign Minister told me. The Europeans have been spectacularly successful in their objective of eliminating war between themselves. For the first time in its history, Europeans have not been at war with one another for fifty years.

The growth of the European Union has not been without friction as the Europeans have taken on the thorny problems of creating a closer political union among countries as different as Portugal and Germany. For instance, the success of their single currency required jettisoning the previously sacrosanct rule of unanimity, the hallmark of EU agreements. Three countries (Great Britain, Denmark, and Sweden) refused to replace their currencies, and the euro was launched without them. Also, the first attempt at designing a treaty to serve as the European Union's "constitution" fell spectacularly apart in the spring of 2005.

We would do well to remember, however, that European countries have an age-old tradition of confronting each other, and that is not something that can be put aside in fifty years. It is a miracle they have managed to get to where they are today, bearing in mind where they started from. "We are now in the process of this loud debate, it is very European, makes a lot of noise, but in the end we will reach an agreement," Palacio told me.

Not everyone, however, is convinced the Europeans will ever succeed in their attempts at political cohesion. James Baker III lived through the debacle of the European Union's first attempt to craft a European security response to the breakup of Yugoslavia. The Europeans appeared eager to take the lead to stop this conflict in their backyard, and the Americans, represented by then Secretary of State Baker, were happy to oblige. What happened? "Like a covey of quail they split and went every which way," Baker said. It is this kind of behavior that leads a lot of people to continue being pessimistic that there will ever be political union.

This kind of skepticism carries over to the practical difficulties of forging a common foreign policy. Because Europe consists of a whole series of sophisticated and ancient nation-states that have different perspectives, the question of a common security and foreign policy is likely to end in total disagreement, or in a very bland policy. "The relationship with the Gulf is different between Britain and the Gulf than between Italy and the Gulf; the relationship with Iraq is different between France and Iraq and the Netherlands and Iraq, and sometimes it will be very difficult to reach a compromise on those issues," John Major told me.

Former President George H. W. Bush, however, held a more optimistic opinion. "Of course, the Europeans are in the process of trying to forge a common understanding about security and foreign policy," he said. "So it's important for the United States to participate in the dialogue from the beginning, which will ensure that America is treated as the ally that it is and not a competitor."

In 2003, the European Union split over support for the American-led invasion of Iraq. As discussed earlier, several of the newer members decided to back the United States while the rest of the European Union, led by France, opposed the invasion. "Chirac scolding angers nations that back U.S." was the headline of a front-page article by Craig Smith in the *New York Times* on February 19, 2003. "We thought we were preparing for war with Saddam Hussein and not Jacques Chirac," the article's author quoted Alexandr Vondra, deputy Foreign Minister of the Czech Republic—one of the recent EU entrants.[5]

Can the integration of Europe ever lead to a United States of Europe? The answer must be that we won't know for a while. But, in my opinion, it would be a mistake to say no.

Skeptics point out that Europe consists of ancient states, each with its own history, culture, and language. They point to the virtually impossible task of transforming this diverse continent into one political entity. But there is a recent successful example of a continent with equal or greater diversity being transformed into one country. Contrary to popular belief, India has existed as one country only since 1947. For centuries before that, a substantial part of the subcontinent of India was composed of independent kingdoms. These sovereign states had their own currencies, military forces, transportation networks, and postal systems. Traveling from Kashmir in the north of India to Chennai (previously Madras) in the south, one will encounter as many races, cultures, and languages as one would find were one to travel in Europe from Scandinavia to Spain.

Skeptics will again raise their voices and say, "But India is an exceptional case. British colonialism inspired and forced the idea of nationhood among the peoples of the Indian subcontinent. No such external shock is contemplated for Europe." The eminent historian Professor James Chace would have begged to disagree. He told me that external shocks have lubricated Europe's integration at many critical milestones. These shocks have come from American actions that were perceived by Europeans as contrary to the behavior expected from a close ally.

In 1956, Egypt nationalized the Suez Canal, in which Britain and France were sizable investors, and for whom the loss of this passageway had serious geopolitical consequences. The two European powers labeled Egypt's action an act of war and invaded Egypt to take back the Canal forcibly. The United States disagreed with the British-French action, publicly voiced its disapproval, and forced a reversal of their invasion. That America would act against two of its closest allies, and force them to reverse a decision they considered to be in their national interests, was a rude awakening for Britain and France and for Europeans in general. Chace reminded me that the landmark treaties resulting in the European Atomic Energy Community and the European Economic Community were signed the very next year in 1957.

Mounting American budget deficits, a stagnant economy, inflation, and the dollar's gyrations played havoc with European currencies in the early 1990s. Since the trade of most European states is with one another, these currency fluctuations were hugely damaging to European economies. The realization that even America could so badly manage its economy, and the effects of this mismanagement on Europe's many, relatively smaller, currencies and markets, were, Chace pointed out, the impetus for the agreement on European monetary and economic union, the centerpiece of the Treaty of Maastricht in 1993. To minimize future currency shocks, Maastricht created a Europe-wide financial market with a powerful single European currency to try and offset the global influence of the dollar.

The Cuban missile crisis of the 1960s had already shown the Europeans that seemingly isolated developments in the American hemisphere had the potential to drag Europe into a nuclear war with the Soviet Union. In 1962, the Soviets had secretly installed nuclear missiles in Cuba, and the United States gave an ultimatum to Russia that if the missiles were not removed, the United States would bomb Cuba. Had that happened, the Soviets would have retaliated by bombing a major European city, probably West Berlin. Under NATO agreements an attack on Europe would trigger an immediate American missile attack on the Soviet Union, which would then have launched a massive missile attack on the United States and Europe. Fortunately for the world, the Russians backed down in Cuba. But the lesson was not lost on the Europeans.[6]

The 2003 unilateral American invasion of Iraq has generated virtually universal European opposition, and it is the latest reminder for Europeans that they need to begin controlling their own security and foreign policy. To achieve this, the Constitutional treaty aims to establish a European Foreign Minister and a European military establishment. These are areas the European states have previously jealously guarded as their own. If Chace's logic holds, as I believe it will, the shock from the Iraqi debacle will also lubricate the treaty's ratification.

In contrast to Napoleon's concept of a European superstate, Jean Monnet dreamt of a unified Europe that would come into being through a pooling of economic resources and markets. All else—joint military planning, a political directorate, a European parliament—would, he maintained, follow.[7] Monnet's dream of a unified Europe is today closer than ever to being realized.

Is the European Union's continued development in America's national interest? "It is in Europe's national interest," Palacio retorted when I asked her the question, "America is an ally and a friend, but it is not involved in the process," she added emphatically. In a sense, this question is moot, the train having already left the station.

That the European Union is a major global player and, in many and growing number of areas, an equal of the United States, is a phenomenon that most Americans do not fully understand or appreciate. John

Major told me he is not even sure American administrations have understood the sheer complexity of the European Union.

There are times when American behavior toward the European Union
borders on the childish. Let me illustrate with a personal anecdote.

In May 2003, two months into the Iraqi war, the Foreign Policy Association held its annual dinner, a glittering black-tie event at which the
guests of honor, United States Secretary of State Colin Powell and his
EU counterpart, Javier Solana, were to speak on the importance of the
transatlantic alliance. America and Europe had engaged in a bitter and
divisive debate at the United Nations, and the guests at this dinner
looked at the event as a timely and unusually important fence-mending
opportunity.

Flanked by the U.S. and EU flags, the band of the U. S. Military
Academy at West Point struck up a resounding version of the "Star-
Spangled Banner," and the assembled guests rose to their feet. As the last
note of the anthem faded, many guests turned to the EU flag to await the
opening bars of the "Ode to Joy" from Beethoven's Ninth Symphony—
the European Union's anthem. The customary short pause before the
anthem gave way to a longer pause, and then the West Point band sat
down. The European Union's national anthem was not to be played that
evening—the United States does not officially recognize it. I later learned
that it would have been permissible to play a recording of the anthem,
an equally insulting choice the Europeans had politely waived. No
doubt, somewhere deep within the U.S. Department of State, or perhaps
the Defense Department, is an official who can explain why it was
acceptable to display the flag of the European Union but improper to
play the anthem associated with it.

Why this lack of attention to, and engagement with, one of the most
significant geopolitical developments of our time? A development that
has changed the political and economic map of Europe, and the way
Europeans think of themselves, their place in the wider world, and the
nature of the European-American relationship.

One explanation is that Americans are an insular people. Complicated geopolitical developments hold little interest for most of them.
And, to be sure, the announcements and jargon that sometimes comes
from the European Union's Brussels bureaucracy are guaranteed to put
even the most dedicated policy wonk to sleep.

I am not sure this explanation holds water, however. An American
president and administration can certainly focus policy by diverting attention to a part of the world or a specific event, and so rouse the interest of
Americans. The genocide in Rwanda could continue unchecked because
it was, arguably, not made an American priority by the Clinton administration. The tragedy in Darfur, Sudan, has been on the front pages of

American newspapers precisely because the Bush administration decided that it had to be an American priority and gave it sustained attention. Attention could easily have been directed to the issue of the integration of Europe, its impact on American foreign policy, and the transatlantic alliance, but it wasn't.[8]

Power politics has also played a part in the American neglect of the European Union. Why give it the recognition it merits, if it might only ensure the success of a potential competitor? After all, who knows what an integrated Europe, with its own currency, military, and security policies might mean for America's traditional role as leader of the Western alliance?

The French Defense Minister, speaking about the impact of a European military arm, captured this power-conundrum when he said, "That will make for a difficult relationship with the United States . . . because at the same time as the United States would like the burden to be better shared, as they often say . . . at present they clearly have very close political control over the alliance as a whole, and they do not want to give it up."[9]

To a large extent, however, this neglect of European integration is a result, in my opinion, of viewing the European Union's successes and failures through Anglo-tinted glasses, through the filter of America's "special relationship" with Britain.

As an illustration of this attitude, consider the widespread lack of attention in the United States to the strategic importance of the euro's introduction. The British government had decided not to adopt the euro but to keep its pound sterling. To win this domestic battle, important British political leaders—Margaret Thatcher, for instance—spoke on both sides of the Atlantic about the ostensible flaws in the very concept of the euro: why it would never come to be and, were it to ever become a reality, why it would not last very long before it imploded.[10]

That the euro and European economic and monetary union would totally transform the European business landscape and create a range of business threats, but also new opportunities, was virtually ignored by most American corporations, government leaders, and the media. The British were America's bridge to Europe. Surely, if they refused to adopt the euro, there must be something wrong with it, and it would never get off the ground. This was the prevailing American attitude. Asked for a comment on the euro's benefits, the best that official Washington could do was to say that if it was good enough for Europe, it was good enough for America.

Less than one year before the euro's launch, the World Affairs Council of Washington, DC, and I organized a conference at the United States Department of State to look at the business and policy implications of the euro. To their credit, a phalanx of Clinton administration officials participated. Ambassador David Aaron, then Under-Secretary of International Trade at the Commerce Department raised quite a few eyebrows with his frank admission that to the best of his knowledge it was the *first* conference in Washington on this critical development!

Britain has had, and continues to have, a love-hate relationship with an integrated Europe—it did not even join the European Economic Community until 1973, twenty years after the European Coal and Steel Community was established. Winston Churchill clearly saw the benefits of a unified Europe—he felt there would be no limits to the happiness, prosperity, and glory of its 400 million people. But he did not envision Britain as a part of it. Britain and the British Commonwealth of Nations were to continue as separate entities.[11]

Churchill left Britons with a dazzling vision. In Churchill's view, post–World War II Britain was to be at the center of three concentric circles: a Europe that would unite; a Commonwealth and empire that would cohere; and a United States that would serve as Britain's partner, the so called "special relationship."[12] Europe began to unite rapidly, and the empire and Commonwealth were soon gone. Because strategically Britain did not see itself as a full partner in the new Europe, it was left with only one of Churchill's concentric circles: the "special relationship" with the United States.

Dean Acheson was unusually prescient in recognizing the importance of Europe's integration and the dangers for Britain *and* the United States in exaggerating the nature of their "Special Relationship."

Acheson believed that Britain made her greatest geopolitical mistake of the postwar period by refusing to join in negotiating the Schuman plan. "From the bitter fruits of this mistake both Britain and Europe are still suffering," Acheson said years later.[13]

By trying to understand and analyze the European Union through Anglo-tinted glasses, the United States has imported this British-European disconnect into its own foreign policy. By interpreting the "special-relationship" between Britain and the United States as the sine qua non of American foreign policy vis-à-vis Europe, the United States has not done any favors to Britain, Europe, or to itself. There is no question that a unique relationship exists between Britain and America. Their shared language and history ensure that. "But unique did not mean affectionate," Acheson observed, reminding his readers that the United States had fought England as an enemy as often as it had fought by England's side as an ally.

Britain has always had a lukewarm interest in joining or promoting the development of the European Union. Today, one of the principal reasons it gives for this attitude is the idea that Britain has an "Anglo-Saxon" culture of free markets and capitalism, while the Europeans still believe in managed economies. That may well be true, but this was not always the objection used by Britain to oppose whole-hearted support of European integration. For instance, its refusal to join the European Coal and Steel Community was justified by Britain for exactly the *opposite* reason. Britain's then-governing Labour Party could not imagine joining the new European free market in coal and steel. The ruling Party's platform and Britain's direction at the time was to construct a state-controlled economy and implement a socialist agenda. There was no way Britain's socialist agenda would let decisions on British coal and steel production be turned over to this new free-market European invention.

Britain's refusal "was not the last chance for Britain to enter Europe, but it was the first wrong choice," Acheson said. Additionally, in view of Britain's reliance on the "special relationship" and its long-running competition with France, the British government could not have been overjoyed to hear President Truman describe the Schuman proposal as "[a]n act of constructive statesmanship and a demonstration of French leadership in the solution of the problems of Europe . . . in the great French tradition."[14]

This French-British struggle for European leadership has been a recurring feature of the European Union since its inception. When the European Economic Community was launched in 1958, Britain, once again, stayed away. Not only did it not join the EEC, but in 1960, Britain helped launch a rival pan-European trade organization called the European Free Trade Association (EFTA). EFTA aimed to achieve the economic integration of Europe, but without the political integration implied by the EEC. EFTA also relied on voluntary participation by sovereign states, rather than the formal treaties that the EEC required.

When it became obvious that EFTA was a failure—most of its members had joined the EEC—Britain turned around and applied for membership in the EEC, only to have its membership vetoed by France. The Europeans, led by France, had started to resent Britain's less than sterling enthusiasm for European integration. To some extent the Europeans also felt Britain's "special relationship" with the United States would allow American influence to creep into internal European affairs.

This analysis of Britain's less than enthusiastic support for the European Union is also supported by some of my interlocutors' observations that the transatlantic divide of 2003 had less to do with differences over the Iraqi war than it does with the competition between France and Britain for Europe's leadership.

The dangers Acheson foresaw in Britain overemphasizing its "special relationship" with the United States, in lieu of its role as a full member and leader of Europe, may well have reached its zenith with Britain's unflinching support for the American decision to invade Iraq in March 2003.

Why would Britain, America's closest ally, the coinventor of modern Iraq, with intimate knowledge of, and deep historical ties to, the Middle East, and with its powerful understanding of Arabs and Islam, not have influenced its American ally's actions more wisely?

Acheson would have immediately understood why it was not in Britain's best interest to offer this wise counsel. Addressing a student conference at the U.S. Military Academy, West Point, in 1962, he presciently said, "Great Britain has lost an empire and has not yet found a role. The attempt to play a separate power role, that is, a role apart from Europe, a role based primarily on a 'special relationship' with the United States, . . . is about played out."[15]

Had Acheson's observation about Britain's largely self-serving and illusory "special relationship" with the United States dictated the formulation of American-European foreign policy, the United States would have taken a different and more balanced European tack in its approach to crafting transatlantic policy, and not lost the opportunity to develop the "special relationship" that really matters today: with the European Union.

It takes two hands to clap, and it goes without saying that the United States used the image and glow of this "special relationship" to manage American public support for the Iraqi invasion. Count me on the side of those who believe it would have been very difficult, if not impossible, for the Bush administration to launch the Iraqi invasion had Britain not supported it. I suspect a coalition of the United States and Azerbaijan might have sounded a bit suspicious to most Americans.

Americans have a sentimental attraction for the British, as they well should. It was after all at one time the mother country, but the continuing foreign-policy tilt towards Britain and away from Europe's center of gravity—the European Union—is yet another reason this transatlantic rift has become a divide.

On July 25, 2002, the Coal and Steel Community's agreement expired, its remaining functions being absorbed by the European Union's executive—the European Commission. Writing in the *Financial Times* on April 18, 2004, Daniel Dombey observed that, "The community, one of the first forerunners of today's European Union, was forged in a world where coal and iron were mainstays of the economy—particularly when war machines needed arming." He continued, "[O]ne of the chief reasons for binding the two industries together . . . was to stop France and Germany from ever entering into combat with each other again." This and more it accomplished, in spades.

It is today worth recalling that of the four men who were most responsible for launching the European Union—Schuman, Monnet, Acheson, and Truman—two were American.

CHAPTER SIX

Business: The Ties That Still Bind

If the political side were to turn really sour, there might be domestic pressures in Europe to treat the United States more as a competitor than as an ally.

—Ambassador Hugo Paemen

There is one aspect of the transatlantic relationship that is thriving. European-American business ties have never been stronger. Transatlantic business is better than it has ever been and continues its upward trajectory even as the political ties deteriorate.

The $3 trillion transatlantic business relationship employs around eight million people—just about as many Americans work for European firms as Europeans do for American ones—and is the biggest and deepest commercial relationship between two continents in recorded history. In spite of the rift over Iraq and America's disdain for Europe's discomfort with the idea of spreading democracy at the point of a sword, the United States invested over $100 billion into the European Union in 2003 and another $92 billion during 2004, a year in which Europe invested $53 billion in the United States. Europe's investment in America doubled between 1998 and 2005 from $518 billion to over a trillion dollars. Europe accounts for around 75 percent of all foreign investment in the United States.[1]

Business with China and India and the commercial benefits of the North American Free Trade Agreement (NAFTA) may make all the headlines, but when one looks at the sheer size of the European-American commercial ties, there is simply no comparison. For instance, American affiliates in Germany alone employed 385,000 manufacturing workers in 2002, which is 80 percent more than the *total* number of manufacturing workers employed in China by United States affiliates. Tiny Switzerland by itself accounted for at least six and a half percent of total United States overseas affiliate[2] earnings ($43.77 billion), which is four times that of earnings in China and twenty-three times that of earnings in India. Although China could well grow into the future predicted for it and become the world's dominant market at some point, for now American companies earn three times as much in Ireland than in China. There is more European investment in Texas alone than the total of American investment in Japan and China put together.[3]

In 2003, after the American invasion of Iraq, American-French relations were at an all time low in the wake of France's role in fomenting and leading European opposition to United States' policy vis-à-vis Iraq. American popular response to France's opposition was quick and predictable. Congressional dining rooms in Washington, DC, changed French fries to Freedom Fries, Americans began boycotting French imports, and politicians urged citizens to cease doing business with France. What happened in reality is revealing for the insight it provides into the nature of the transatlantic business link.

In 2004, the year after the American invasion of Iraq, United States imports from France grew to $31.8 billion, the largest they had ever been, and American inward investment in French companies during the same year grew to $6.8 billion, 45 percent larger than American investment in China in the same year. The reverse was equally true. In 2004, French investment in the United States almost doubled from the previous year to $9 billion; even the Germans, who opposed the United States invasion of Iraq just as much as the French did, wound up investing $6.8 billion in America during 2004, *twenty times* more than they had in 2003.[4]

This is an incredible vote of confidence in each other by America and Europe, and I count myself in the camp of those who believe the transatlantic alliance's disintegration would have proceeded at a much faster rate without these deep commercial bonds. "Fortunately, trade has served as an important anchor for the transatlantic relationship," former President George H. W. Bush told me. And it is a tribute to European and American businesswomen and -men who have been able to see beyond the political storm clouds and keep the business relationship growing even as the political links have been systematically eroding.

In their book *The Transatlantic Economy 2005*, Daniel Hamilton and Joseph Quinlan point out that American firms invested more capital overseas in the 1990s—in excess of $750 billion—than in the prior four decades combined. The bulk of this foreign direct investment went, not to the developing or emerging economies, but to Europe. Why? Because that is where the markets and the profits are, Hamilton and Quinlan explained.

I mentioned earlier that the transatlantic economy directly employs around eight million people. This does not give the full picture, as Hamilton and Quinlan point out. Almost as many jobs are created in the United States and Europe to support those directly employed, and the report estimates the total transatlantic workforce at twelve to fourteen million.

What is more, European investment in the United States is spread across the entire country, and virtually every state benefits from it. European investment in Utah (population, 2.5 million) amounts to $10.9 billion and supports 25,900 jobs. Even in a small state such as Vermont (population 623,000), where the author lives, European investment totals over a billion dollars and supports over 7,900 jobs. In 2004, Europeans purchased $1.1 billion worth of goods from Utah and $313 million worth of goods from Vermont. Interestingly, around 28 percent of the jobs supported by European investment in both Utah and Vermont were in manufacturing, a sector that has been losing jobs to low-cost Asian countries and China for years.[5]

It goes without saying that any damage to the transatlantic business relationship would play havoc with European and American jobs and standards of living. Is the deterioration of this link even remotely possible, given the size, complexity, and momentum of the European-American business relationship?

The answer is Yes, the link can deteriorate, and, in my opinion, the stars are already aligned in that direction. European and American perceptions of each other, globalization, Europe's increasing desire for political independence and commercial diversification, and a rapidly integrating European marketplace are some of the forces pushing against the inertia of the massive existing transatlantic business ties.

Successful businesspeople owe their success to their focus on their company's profitability and long term business strategy. They do not choose customers, partners, or suppliers by using political benchmarks. Political trends may come and go; business interests drive everything. No matter what the political winds may bring, "Commercial relations will in the end continue," Ana Palacio, Spain's former Foreign Minister told me; and she could have just as well have spoken for the American business community when she added, "because we Europeans are used to having commercial relations that have an independent life."

Although this may be generally true, Hugo Paemen, the erstwhile European Union Ambassador to the United States, worries about the creeping damage done by seemingly unimportant public perceptions and private

attitudes unless they are nipped in the bud firmly and quickly. He referred
to the American antagonism towards the French in the lead-up to the Iraqi
war and the call for an American boycott of French goods such as Perrier
mineral water, wines from Bordeaux and Burgundy, and so on. "These are
for the moment marginal elements which don't affect the relationship,"
Paemen, said, "but at the level of public opinion and perception you have
to manage them, it is like a marriage you know, you can be as good for
each other as you can be, but if you don't manage your relationship, you
can fall over a very small thing," he told me.

The Dubai Debacle

The destructive impact of unchecked public perceptions stoked by political opportunism was clearly on display in March 2006 with the undoing
of the Dubai Ports World (DPW) deal.

The government of Dubai, one of the seven kingdoms comprised in
the United Arab Emirates (UAE) in the Middle East–and a staunch
American ally for years–had just acquired a British company called
P&O that ran the terminals at six American seaports including those of
New York and New Jersey. The purchase would have put an Arab
government–owned company in charge of operating these ports. Within
a matter of days what had been a routine business transaction that had
been executed under British laws and vetted under U.S. laws had to be
scuttled because of the post–September 11 perception in America of
Arabs as terrorists. It mattered not that the deal had the approval of the
President of the United States and America's intelligence agencies and
had the overwhelming support of America's business community. Nor
did it matter that another Dubai government–owned company, Inch-
cape Shipping Services, provides maintenance services for U.S. Navy
ships operating in the Middle East, or that Dubai is a close American
ally in the "war on terror," having contributed to the capture of a number of al-Qaida terrorists. Perceptions carried the day. "With midterm
elections approaching, no politician wanted to go home and explain to
voters why a company controlled by the government of Dubai was taking over operations at six U.S. ports–without so much as a meow of protest from Congress," wrote Daren Fonda in the March 9, 2006, issue of
Time. At a speech I attended not long after this episode, Jack Welch, the
former CEO of General Electric and one of America's most accomplished and admired business leaders, called it one of the stupidest decisions he had ever seen.

The stupidity of the decision started to become clear just five months
later, and the move on the international chessboard that was made by

the UAE–of which Dubai is a part–could not have been made without the existence of the euro. The European single currency offered the UAE a geopolitical opening, and they took it.

"The United Arab Emirates' Central Bank Governor has confirmed a strategic decision had been taken to move 10 percent of its foreign exchange reserves into euros," the *Financial Times* of July 14, 2006, reported in a story by Roula Khalaf. Governor Sultan bin Nasser al-Suwaidi also predicted that the Gulf Cooperation Council (GCC), which includes Saudi Arabia, Kuwait, the UAE, Qatar, Bahrain, and Oman, would move from the dollar peg to a floating exchange rate after the introduction of their single currency, planned for 2010.

The U.S. dollar has been the dominant world currency, having displaced the British pound sterling from that title in the 1950s. In 1973, the Organization of Petroleum Exporting Countries (OPEC) quadrupled the price of oil and tied it to the dollar. In practical terms, this means all purchases and sales of oil anywhere in the world are executed in dollars. The world's economy runs on dollars, and this OPEC decision made the U.S. dollar the most desirable and powerful currency in the world. Dollars are hoarded by central banks around the world, and they keep the majority of their reserves in dollar-denominated assets, usually U.S. Treasury Bonds. Because reserves are hoarded, America is able to issue and sell an almost unlimited amount of Treasury paper, which it does, to finance its growing deficit. In a sense it is akin to having the power to write an unlimited amount of checks, secure in the knowledge that they will never be cashed. This is one of the privileges of being the world's only reserve currency.

That privilege ended on January 1, 2000, with the introduction of the euro. Overnight the world acquired a second major currency, and the dollar had a challenger. Nobody expects the euro to dethrone the dollar any time soon, but there is no question that the euro brought with it a powerful diversification option for central banks. The Central Bank of the UAE exercised this option when it converted 2.9 billion dollars of its 29 billion dollar reserves into euros.

More than 600 billion dollars are held in the coffers of the oil-producing countries of the Middle-East; Russia, another major oil producer, keeps another 220 billion dollars.[6]

My point is that, until the creation of the euro, these countries had no choice but to hold dollars; no other currency was strong enough to take the risk of holding it for the long term. But the euro, backed by a currency block of about the same size as the United States in terms of gross domestic product and geographical size, is different. The world now has two reserve currencies. This is what makes the decision of the UAE to sell almost three billion dollars and replace them with euros so significant. Before European integration there would have been no choice; now there is.

And what if the GCC, after establishing its own single currency by 2010, were to decide to denominate its oil in euros? What might this do to the dollar? To American foreign policy? To relations with Europe?

All those checks that America thought would never be cashed would be presented for payment, and the dollar would drop significantly in value and even more significantly in prestige. Might such a decision be the weapon of choice for Arab and Muslim countries that resent America's perceived high-handed, imperial behavior?

For those who find this hypothesis far-fetched, I would refer them to Johns Hopkins University–trained information security analyst William Clark, who has argued that one of the reasons for the American invasion of Iraq was Saddam Hussein's decision in 2000 that Iraq would henceforth accept only euros for its oil in the United Nations "Oil-For-Food" program.[7] Clark hammers home his argument by pointing out that after America toppled Saddam Hussein, the first tender for sale of Iraqi oil reverted back to dollars. He quotes from the *Financial Times*: "The tender, for which bids are due by June 10, switches the transaction back to dollars–the international currency of oil sales–despite the greenback's recent fall in value. Saddam Hussein in 2000 insisted Iraq's oil be sold for euros, a political move, but one that improved Iraq's recent earnings thanks to the rise in the value of the euro against the dollar."[8]

Clark leaves us with a troubling thought: "In essence, Iran is about to commit a far greater offense than Saddam Hussein's conversion to the euro for Iraq's oil exports in the fall of 2000. Beginning in March 2006, the Tehran government has plans to begin competing with New York's NYMEX and London's IPE with respect to international oil trades–using a euro-based international oil-trading mechanism. The proposed Iranian oil bourse signifies that without some sort of US intervention, the euro is going to establish a firm foothold in the international oil trade."[9]

Iran did in fact move forward to grant a license for the euro-denominated market on May 5, 2006. To be fair, it is not at all certain the market will take off, as the *Toronto Globe and Mail* pointed out in an AP report on the license award. "Iran is not a very attractive site for a market, given the volatile nature of its politics, the U.S. sanctions against it and the lack of a fair legal system. Moreover, there is no indication that the European Union is interested in vying to become the world's central bank."[10] The point remains that it could happen, and all of this because of Europe's new single currency.

Monetary Friction, Political Friction:
The Vicious Cycle

As the euro continues to become a stronger currency, its potential to serve as a dollar replacement will grow in attractiveness. Governments will choose to diversify their foreign currency holdings, rebalancing the amounts of dollars and euros they hold to increase the proportion of euro holdings. The impact of this shift in the global monetary balance cannot but sour American public opinion against the Europeans. Politicians and the media will see to that: none of this would have happened, they will say, if those Europeans had not introduced their euro. The increased political friction will have to seep into the business side—yet another question mark for those who believe the transatlantic business ties will continue growing and strengthening forever.

"Sure, absolutely," is how James Baker, former United States Treasury Secretary answered my query about the chances of the transatlantic rift seeping into the business relationship. Paul Volcker, former Chairman of the Federal Reserve Board, agreed.

Volcker spoke about the "integrating force of technology on the business side and the disintegrating force on the political side," and wondered how it would balance out. He speculated that one fallout from this tension might be an increase in the level of regionalism.

Europe has set up the European Union with its common currency, the United States of course has its common currency, the Gulf Cooperation Council is scheduled to have its common currency by 2010, "eventually Asia will have a common currency, and you won't have the same perception of a common interest," Volcker told me. Everyone will be "big, fat, and happy within their own borders"; the lack of a common interest will be reflected economically, and "you will get these big swings in exchange rates that don't have any economic rationale but are a real hindrance to international business, which then drives them more and more into regional arrangements."

The end result of this vicious cycle, according to Volcker, is "less and less interest in world trade organizations, less interest in global trade agreements such as the already faltering Doha Round, less interest in multilateralism, and yet more interest in regionalism."

The point I feel that both Paemen and Volcker are trying to make is that bigger problems happen if small problems and perceptions are left to themselves. Just because business leaders want to operate on a separate track from political trends does not mean they will have the luxury to do so. "Things do not get better just because you leave them alone, they normally get worse," Senator Chuck Hagel told me. "We are going to constantly have to work through these issues and be mindful of the relationships that are important for our future."

The Challenge of the Globally Integrated Enterprise

Absent a vibrant transatlantic alliance, the inexorable march of globalization is another threat to the strings that bind Europe and America in their incredible business arrangement. This threat, in my opinion, comes from the continuing evolution of the modern corporation under the influence of globalization and technology and the effect of this evolution on mutual European-American business investment.

Contrary to popular belief, outsourcing has not yet made the dent in European and American jobs that headlines would have it. In reality, actual statistics paint a very different picture. The bulk of corporate America's overseas workforce does not toil in low-wage nations such as Mexico and China. Most foreigners working for U. S. companies abroad are employed in the industrialized nations, notably Europe. The same is true for European companies. Despite stories on the continent about home-grown European companies decamping for cheap labor markets in Eastern Europe or Asia, most foreigners working for European companies outside the European Union are American.[11]

This little-known fact about the European-American business relationship is another example of why it will take an enormous shift in the way business is done to corrode and weaken the transatlantic business link. However, the shift in how business is conducted is now well under way.

Writing in the journal *Foreign Affairs,* Samuel Palmisano, Chairman of the Board, President, and Chief Executive Officer of IBM, explained: "A new corporate entity based on collaborative innovation, integrated production, and outsourcing to specialists is emerging in response to globalization and new technology."[12] Such "Globally Integrated Enterprises," as he calls this latest evolution in the nature of the modern corporation, will "end up reshaping geopolitics, trade, and education." It is this Globally Integrated Enterprise that poses a powerful challenge to the existing cozy transatlantic business arrangement.

To understand the nature of this challenge, it is important to note two facts about the transatlantic business relationship. First, recall the reason Hamilton and Quinlan give for the enormous size of the European-American business relationship: "because that is where the markets and profits are." Europe and America remain each other's main source of global profits.[13] Couple this with the fact that foreign direct investment (factories, subsidiaries, sales affiliates) reveal more about the depth of a business relationship than the much simpler "trade statistics" that are normally used to describe global business.[14]

Until recently, companies generally chose to produce goods close to where they sold them; the cost of long supply lines did not make much sense in these markets. "As a consequence, most foreign investments targeted specific foreign markets. Today "companies are investing more to change the way they supply the entire global market. The global integration of production cuts costs and taps new sources of skills and knowledge,"

Palmisano wrote. Standardization of manufacturing processes, software, and communications protocols has severed the link between where a product or service is produced and where it is consumed. The Internet has eliminated distance and time and made it possible to use local talent and sourcing of raw material (be it precision-manufactured goods or brainpower) to assemble the product or service anywhere for delivery wherever it is needed. It is now cost-effective to produce the components that go into an item anywhere in the world and then put them together in a mass assembly center such as China. At a recent visit to a retail store in New York I noticed a pair of scissors labeled "Made in India, Germany, and Bangladesh"!

No wonder Palmisano says that state borders define less and less the boundaries of corporate thinking or practice. He estimates that between 2000 and 2003, foreign firms, including European chemical companies, and United States industrial conglomerates, built 60,000 manufacturing plants in China.[15]

Whether the 2020 edition of *The Transatlantic Economy* will still tell us that American firms hire mostly Europeans and European firms hire mostly Americans is an open question. As the Globally Integrated Enterprise spreads, transatlantic jobs will increasingly slip away to other shores, and the business ties that bind Europe and America will continue to weaken—even more reason to not let the political alliance drift away.

Galileo: Europe Finds Its Own Position

As Europe's economy continues its evolution into a seamless continental economy like that of the United States, it will increasingly be able to undertake research and investment in intensive high-technology commercial projects of the kind now dominated by the United States. The strategic nature of these projects and their commercial potential will attract investment from other countries who want to diversify their investment portfolio beyond the United States. The Galileo positioning system is a project that illustrates this development.

Literally out of the blue, America's Global Positioning System (GPS) has become an indispensable tool. It can be used to pinpoint a position on earth to within 10 meters (33 feet), and incredibly, GPS navigation signals fall to earth like rainwater or sunlight and can be used by anyone at no cost. No wonder the uses of GPS have mushroomed over the last decade. With GPS, cars navigate, hikers locate their whereabouts, fishermen navigate to fish shoals, the United States Air Force's "smart" bombs find their way into the windows of terrorists' houses. U.S. Army troops are deployed in combat with a "Blue Force Tracker" GPS transmitter on their helmets so their movement, and that of their unit can be tracked on digital maps. Soon the technology will be ubiquitous in cell phones, wristwatches, cameras, and bicycles. Indeed, anything that moves is a potential user of GPS technology—and so are many things that stay put, which can use GPS as an extremely precise clock.[16] Commercial revenues from the application of GPS technology exceeded $12 billion in 2002 and were growing at an annual rate of more than 20 percent.[17]

Developed by the U.S. Department of Defense, GPS relies on a cluster of twenty-four satellites that circle the earth at an altitude of 12,000 miles in varying orbits that allow multiple satellites to be seen from any location; signals from at least three satellites are required for accuracy. The satellites began to be launched by the Department of Defense in 1978, and the American taxpayer has spent over $20 billion to bring the system to its current state of usefulness and accuracy.

With GPS, America dominates the world of satellite navigation and, by proxy, the enormous commercial and military business that has developed around it. It is a strategic-commercial monopoly unlike any other, because every GPS device in the world, whether it is military or commercial, relies on the United States to keep working. It is as if every light bulb in the world were powered by electricity generated in America.

But America's GPS monopoly is less than four years away from ending, because the European Union expects by 2010 to have launched all thirty satellites and set up the ground control infrastructure of its own space-based navigation system, Galileo.

Galileo is a civilian-controlled enterprise, unlike its American counterpart which is controlled by the Department of Defense. Galileo is designed to generate revenue to support its operations, whereas GPS is funded by the United States government. As accurate as GPS is, it uses decades-old technology and so is not accurate enough for many applications such as airplane landing systems. This technology gap will not exist in Galileo, whose accuracy is projected to be as low as one centimeter (less than half an inch) as compared to GPS's one meter (a little over three feet).

Why, it might be asked, given the enormous transatlantic business relationship, would the Europeans want to make the large investment necessary to create a satellite navigation system of their own when they can use GPS at no cost? The answer has political, strategic, military, and commercial dimensions and sheds more light on the transformation of the transatlantic business relationship.

The Europeans first became aware of GPS-controlled weaponry during the 1999 phase of the Kosovo conflict, when NATO forces fought the armed forces of Yugoslavia. In this war, as in the first Gulf War, air power was widely used to limit military casualties to a bare minimum.

The "smart" bombs available for use in Kosovo by the United States were guided to their targets using laser technology, a system whose operations are affected by weather. Bad weather during the early stages of the Kosovo conflict severely restricted the bombs' laser guidance systems. For instance, out of the first 21 days of the conflict, air power could be fully used for only seven. The U.S. Air Force responded by accelerating its plans to integrate GPS guidance systems into the "smart" bombs.[18]

This was the first major use of GPS in conflict, and it gave the Europeans a chance to observe first-hand what the military technology of tomorrow would look like. The Europeans also became aware of the gap that existed between European and American military capabilities.

On their side, the Americans made sure the Europeans did not forget the real meaning of this deficit. "We pulled off the Kosovo caper through fortuitous circumstances, bombing the Serbs back to their country for just two aircraft lost (both pilots were recovered unhurt)," one U.S. official said.[19]

It was not long before the Europeans realized two other and potentially more significant implications of America's monopoly of GPS: the United States could simply turn off the GPS signals in any geographic area if it so desired. Even if the Europeans developed their own GPS-guided weaponry, the United States could disable them all by shutting off GPS signals during a battle of which it did not approve. Also, the ratio of civilian to military users was growing rapidly. In 2003, there were a hundred civilian users for every military user, which meant that the commercial losses for European firms from not being able to access GPS could be substantial.[20]

European feelings were captured in a speech by French President Jacques Chirac in a speech to the National Center for Space Studies in Paris in December 2001, when he declared that "The United States spends six times more public money on the space sector than Europe. Failure to react would inevitably lead to our countries becoming first scientific and technological vassals, then industrial and economic vassals."[21]

Interestingly, the Galileo project had stalled in European bureaucracy over funding issues. It got a new lease on life in 2002 partly because of American pressure to kill the project. Almost as soon as the European Union announced the Galileo project in 1999, the United States tried to derail it with a variety of arguments. Sure, Galileo would be more accurate than America's GPS, but GPS was already in place, available for free, and scheduled for technical upgrades, so why duplicate expenses? "The United States sees no compelling need for Galileo," huffed Ralph Braibanti, the State Department official leading talks with the European Union on the project.[22] Later the American arguments shifted to a security theme, with U.S. Deputy Secretary of Defense Paul Wolfowitz warning the

Europeans about the "security ramifications for future NATO operations" if Europe proceeded with the Galileo project.[23] The American pressure (motivated, in the European view, simply by fear of losing a monopoly), served only to lubricate the wheels of European cohesion around Galileo. In February 2002 Germany, the key holdout, came on board. "Satellite navigation is one of the key technologies of the future . . . of considerable political, strategic and economic importance," German Transport Minister Kurt Bodewig said in Berlin.[24] Galileo was on its way.

The commercial benefits of Galileo include the creation of over 100,000 technology-related jobs in Europe resulting from an investment exceeding $4 billion.[25] But that is just the beginning. All the evidence points to Galileo not only leapfrogging over GPS technologically but becoming a commercial success as investment flows into it from other countries and user revenue streams begin to kick in.

In 2003, China announced that it will invest $259 million in the Galileo satellite tracking system. Of special interest to China was the fact that Galileo will be a civilian-run operation that will be guaranteed in all but the direst circumstances, so services that are critical to safety—landing planes, for example—can rely on the data.[26]

In July 2004, Israel signed an agreement with the European Union to become a partner in Galileo. In 2005, India, Ukraine, Morocco, and Saudi Arabia joined the project. In 2006, South Korea joined Galileo, and other countries including Canada, Mexico, Pakistan, Brazil, and Russia were seriously considering doing so.[27]

Galileo is but one of a number of instances in which the United States has led the world in high-technology strategic sectors only to see the European Union come from behind and either catch up or pass America by. Witness the European Ariane rocket project, which now has half the global market for commercial space launches, and EADS, the European consortium that manufactures the ubiquitous Airbus series of passenger aircraft, which has ended Boeing's monopoly of the civilian airplane business.

As important as transatlantic ties are, they are in transition. Two decades ago the United States led the pace in virtually every high-growth technology sector relative to Europe. That is far less true now, indicating that the business ties will become much more balanced in the future. While it will take a while, given the strength and dynamic nature of the American economy and the still evolving integration of Europe's markets at this time, the direction clearly favors increasingly effective competition, and more opportunity to diversify from the historically massive European-American relationship. Although the business ties are deep and resilient, their transformation will continue to make them less of a brake on the downward slide in the European-American political relationship.

CHAPTER SEVEN

La Solidarité des Faits: A New Agenda

We need to revitalize the transatlantic alliance and restore it, and we need to recognize that there is fault on both sides here, and that we cannot let our disappointment cloud our judgment about the importance of going forward.

—Former U.S. Secretary of State and Secretary of the Treasury James A. Baker III

Robert Schuman, the visionary founder of the European Union, conceived what, in hindsight, was a fail-safe technique for the integration of Europe. He realized there were overriding reasons for European countries to join together and create a larger political and economic entity, but he recognized the odds were against such an enterprise succeeding. Centuries of war, conquests, prejudices, not to mention the blood-soaked Nazi era which had just ended, made the project a near-impossible task. Schuman had the vision to realize that if the project did get going, the intrinsic advantages of the idea would move it along with greater and greater momentum, and nothing would be able to stop it.

"*La solidarité des faits*"–tangible projects that create tangible solidarity– was his way forward. Ana Palacio, Spain's Foreign Minister, succinctly summarized Schuman's vision and his creativity during two illuminating conversations. "The European approach is all about overcoming divides; indeed, Europe is based on the biggest of all divides, centuries of bloody wars between Europeans," she told me. "The European way is to acknowledge the divide but put it aside, and then create common ground on which to build specific projects. Then you revisit the rift, assess it, and overcome it."

I have suggested that the current rift between the transatlantic partners is fundamentally different from past ones, and it won't just mend itself with time or even a change in personalities. It is time to review the foundation that supports the alliance and make the necessary modifications to adapt it to today's geopolitical realities. It seems to me that Schuman's strategy–focus on tangible projects to create tangible solidarity–offers a proven formula for success in bridging the transatlantic divide. This strategy will buy time, let hot heads cool down, and replace the currently fashionable but misguided objective of *repairing the rift* with a more realistic and attainable objective of creating an *ever-closer alliance.*

I count myself in the camp of those who believe an American-European alliance is indispensable to meet the challenges of the twenty-first century, but there are those who take a different, more jaundiced view of its value to the United States. The mainly Republican neoconservatives question whether the European Union's continued growth is in America's national interest, and they would prefer an American policy that actively promotes discord within the European Union's member states to weaken the Union. They would like the United States "[t]o acknowledge that a more clearly integrated Europe is no longer an unqualified American interest, force European governments to choose between Paris and Washington and do our utmost to preserve Britain's strategic independence from Europe."[1] Fortunately, many of their equally conservative but clearer-thinking Republican brethren disapprove of this anti-European policy. "The enlargement of the European Union is a good thing for the United States . . . the greater integration will strengthen Europe, the United States and the transatlantic relationship," former President George H. W. Bush told me.

In my opinion, these more realistic Republicans, along with all but one of the people I interviewed, believe that a policy of trying to divide the Europeans, if it is adopted by the United States, will make rapprochement with the Europeans virtually impossible. This, in turn, will damage America's long-term security and commercial interests. The onus is on these more internationally focused and clear-headed Republicans to join their Democratic colleagues and construct a bipartisan initiative to forge a new transatlantic alliance.

European countries have spent fifty years willingly giving up increasing amounts of sovereignty to establish an ever-closer union among themselves. For economic reasons, joining the European Union is critically important for its smaller member countries, the ones most susceptible to American pressure and offers of aid. These countries conduct most of their trade within the European Union and are eager to become a part of this expanding area of free trade. They look forward to agricultural and other developmental subsidies from Brussels; they can hardly wait to ditch their Lilliputian currencies for the euro, which, with the United States dollar and the Japanese yen, is now one of the world's three major currencies. They are not about to sacrifice these objectives and become pariahs in their own backyard. This is not to say they will not use America's seductive appeals to negotiate a better power-sharing arrangement within the Union, or use the leverage to strengthen their own transatlantic links; of course they will. But an official American policy of trying to weaken the growth of the European Union is not realistic.

As recent events have demonstrated, the world is now faced with deadly new challenges: The scourge of terrorism, coupled with easy access to weapons of mass destruction; endemic poverty, which consigns most of the world to medieval levels of subsistence while the West enjoys unprecedented wealth; the scourge of AIDS and other deadly diseases; and a growing divide between the West and Islamic countries, are just the most dangerous ones.

The threat from terrorism is equally terrifying and is in many ways more dangerous than was the threat from the Soviet Union during the Cold War. Today's terrorist threat is stateless, and in contrast to the Communist ideology, which at least explained Soviet behavior, there is no clear explanation yet for what drives these terrorists. The Europeans, with their years of experience in combating terrorism, would bring badly needed perspectives and experienced resources to complement America's fight against terrorism.

"It really concerns me that no one is trying to understand the root causes of terrorism," Brent Scowcroft told me. His point is more important than it at first appears. For instance, during the Cold War, nuclear weapons delivery required sophisticated and expensive missile technology, available to only a handful of countries. Today's weapons can be delivered with pinpoint accuracy by suicide bombers: an inexpensive delivery system of limitless and universal availability. What drives this seemingly insane act? Popular American opinion—as reflected in the media—explains this act as an Islamic phenomenon: "The roots of Muslim rage are to be found in Islam itself," David Frum and Richard Perle tell us in *An End To Evil*.[2] Suicide bombing, however, was perfected by the Tamil Tigers of Sri Lanka—who are Hindus, not Muslims. They blew up India's Prime Minister, Rajiv Gandhi, in a 1991 suicide attack, not because the woman who pulled the pin from her grenade thought she would go to heaven, but because the Tamils believed they were engaged in a struggle against tyranny, and India had sent in its army to support their oppressors. In America, the religious explanation is what is widely believed to be the sole driving force behind the suicide bombers, and this in turn leads to simplistic and inaccurate prescriptions to stop this form of terrorism.

The 9/11 Commission pointed out: "New threats can emerge quickly. An organization like Al-Qaida, headquartered in a country on the other side of the earth, in a region so poor that electricity and telephone were scarce, could nevertheless scheme to wield weapons of unprecedented destructive power in the largest cities of the United States."[3]

As a clearly perturbed American Defense Secretary Rumsfeld put it, "The cost-benefit ratio is against us! Our cost is billions against the terrorists' costs of millions."[4] For a cost estimated at under $250,000, the September 11 terrorists inflicted billions of dollars of damage to the American economy, killed upwards of three thousand people, and transformed American society. The cost of a foreign policy that is not well thought out and that ascribes religious explanations to what may in reality be a socioeconomic and political phenomenon is dangerous to American security because it promotes religious bigotry and is hugely expensive at the same time.

In today's world of shadowy terrorists, inexpensive means of global communication, and deadly weapons available to virtually anyone who can pay for them, the incorrect analysis of what constitutes threat takes on a whole different level of complexity. During the Cold War it was possible at least to speak to the Soviet Union, which had a government led by a chief executive who could be reached by telephone. Today's terrorists have neither.

During the Cold War, the threat of mutual destruction was comforting in a way, Palacio said. "The notion of 'I won't attack you because if I do, you will attack and destroy me' created a status quo which is now no longer valid." For Europeans of Palacio's generation the Cold War was defined by a clearly marked border, with planes and soldiers depicted in red on the Soviet side, and in blue on the Western side, with more blue than red. No such border exists today, and even the enemy cannot be clearly identified.

In this complicated, chaotic, and unfamiliar world, it is vital that Europe and America stand together. "Where is the advantage in dismantling the transatlantic alliance?" asked former British Prime Minister Major. "It has been the most successful security relationship that the Western world has ever known." Europe and America have such a community of interests that are not debated or argued about—the war on terror, trade, a whole host of other things including cultural ties—"That it is really important we not let our disappointments cloud our judgment," Baker said.

America's sole superpower status will end some day in the not too distant future. Countries such as China, India, Brazil, and Russia, acting singly and in partnership, will see to that. When that happens, it will be far more beneficial for Europe and America to face a new and uncertain world, and its challenges, with the alliance intact rather than uncoupled.

What follows are suggestions, based on my own ideas, but inspired by the conversations I had for this book, for regenerating a new transatlantic alliance. Execution of this agenda will require continuous engagement between the alliance partners at the highest levels for many years—Schuman's successful recipe for bringing together divergent national interests.

New Global Rules of Engagement

"Nations Seek World Order Centered on U.N., Not U.S.," headlined the *New York Times* on February 19, 2003. Richard Bernstein reported from Brussels that even with the break in EU ranks when eight states backed America's invasion of Iraq, all fifteen EU countries were unanimous on the one point that captures the essence of the transatlantic divide—a commitment to keeping the United Nations at the center of the international order.

"More Americans Now Faulting U.N. on Iraq, Poll Finds—More Than Half in Survey Back U.S. Invasion Even Without Security Council Vote," was the lead story in the *New York Times* just a few weeks later, on March 11, 2003. And a few days later, though unable to convince a majority of the Security Council's membership about the rightness of its course, the United States did exactly that—it bypassed the Security Council and invaded Iraq in what was for all practical purposes a coalition of two: itself and the United Kingdom.

This is not a temporary rift between the United States and Europe. Two and a half years later, in August 2005, when Iran ended its moratorium on uranium conversion against the wishes of France, Germany, Britain, and the United States, President Bush, speaking on August 12 to Israeli television, refused to rule out the use of force as a last resort, "[t]o press the Iranian government to give up its nuclear program." The very next day German Chancellor Gerhard Schroeder voiced his disapproval and insisted that the military option should come off the table. "We have seen it doesn't work," he said in clear reference to America's invasion of Iraq.[5]

These two excerpts from the *New York Times* again illuminate a basic disconnect between Europeans and Americans when it comes to the way a threat is perceived, the importance of acting through multilateral institutions, the use of force, and the effect of the American-led invasion of Iraq. President Bush obviously believed the Iraqi war has been so successful that he left open the possibility of trying another one next door. Chancellor Schroeder believed instead that the Iraqi invasion had not worked. If the alliance is to function effectively again, Europeans and

Americans must reach a compromise on the fundamental issue of when and how to use military power. This thought was succinctly captured by Peter Jay, a former British Ambassador to the United States. He opened the April 2003 Foreign Policy Association/ebizChronicle.com conference at Ditchley with this warning: "Until we, the United States and Europe, sort out agreed basic premises about the rules of the global game, it will become increasingly difficult to resolve, or even indefinitely to fudge the day to day issues that confront us."[6]

In March of 2003, when the Iraqi war was about to begin and emotions were raw, neither side would have contemplated a discussion of such a fundamental issue. But now, with the lessons from Iraq and Afghanistan staring both sides in the face, it is a different story. America must realize it cannot succeed in its quest for a more peaceful and stable world without its traditional European partners, and they, in turn, must recognize the costs, to themselves and the world, of an untethered America. Both sides undoubtedly have a whole new appreciation of the value of the alliance, the need to rebuild it, and the obstacles to doing so.

To move forward with the idea of a European-American agreement on the use of force will require a dialogue on two key issues. First, there must be agreement on the universal values that transcend cultures, because Europe and America will have to fight for them. Second, there must be agreement on the use of force: when is it justified and how should it be used, given that America and Europe do not share the same vision about this.

Even though it creates some frustrations, the hegemony of the United States is tolerable for Europeans, and, by and large, they can live with it. But, with their longer historical perspective, Europeans know the unipolar world of today will not stay that way. "The Roman, Byzantium, and Austro-Hungarian empires have come and gone, China will soon be a superpower, Brazil and India stand in the wings. So wouldn't it be more reassuring for our children and grandchildren if at the moment when the world's power balance changes again we have more established and formalized rules at the international level?" Hugo Paemen, the former EU Ambassador to the United States, asked.

As important as an agreement over the rules of engagement is, it faces three tough roadblocks.

The growing chasm between the Muslim world and the United States makes agreement complicated. From the Middle East to Indonesia, America is despised as never before. From wide support and sympathy after September 11, recent polls showed that "The bottom had fallen out of support for America in most of the Muslim world . . . since last summer [2003], favorable ratings for the United States have fallen from sixty-one percent to fifteen percent in Indonesia and from seventy-one percent to thirty-eight percent in Nigeria."[7] In a Zogby poll of June 2003, 76 percent of Egyptians viewed the United States unfavorably; a year later, in June 2004, Zogby found that number had increased to 98 percent. A Pew Research Center report in March 2004 pointed out that in the predominantly Muslim countries surveyed, anger toward the United States remains pervasive. Osama bin Laden is viewed favorably by large percentages in Pakistan (65 percent), Jordan (55 percent), and Morocco (45 percent). Even in Turkey, where bin Laden is highly unpopular, as many as 31 percent say that suicide attacks against Americans and other Westerners in Iraq are justifiable. Majorities in all four Muslim nations surveyed doubt the sincerity of the war on terrorism. Instead, most say it is an effort to control Mideast oil and to dominate the world. "Two-thirds of the countries from Indonesia to Turkey were very or somewhat fearful that America may attack them." I recently asked the wife of a Middle Eastern diplomat (deliberately but rather injudiciously!) why fundamentalist Muslims appear to consider killing to be an acceptable pursuit. The response was immediate and most uncharacteristic of a diplomat's spouse. "Your fundamentalist Christian president invaded Iraq and killed over a hundred thousand Iraqis, so what is the difference?" Her response certainly brought the state of Islamic-American relations into sharp relief. It is clearly an uphill battle to win Islamic hearts and minds!

The main problem now is that a new and resurgent alliance between Europe and America could be easily perceived by the Muslim world as more proof of the West ganging up against Islam. The European Union's Muslim population now exceeds 15 million, or over 10 percent of the European Union's population. It is not as well integrated into mainstream Europe as America's Muslim population, leaving aside for the moment the deterioration in American Muslims' trust in their government since September 11. In both the European Union and the United States, Islam is the fastest-growing religion, and in both, after September 11, ordinary Muslims feel under pressure with respect to their civil rights. They are increasingly an object of growing prejudice to their fellow citizens.

In Europe the actions of a few extremists have set back the already feeble integration of Muslim immigrants into European society, but, more tragically, the much more successful integration of Muslims into American society has been thrown into reverse. Not too long ago I attended a luncheon meeting at a well-known New York think tank at which the author of a new book on immigrants was the speaker. As part of her research she attended a focus group of Pakistani Muslim women, who were invited to discuss how their lives had changed after the attacks of September 11. The book author was incredulous at the extreme discomfort of these Muslim women when they were told why it was now necessary to treat them differently from other Americans. They were horrified, she said, and calmly went on to tell an approving luncheon crowd that the Pakistani women had better get used to it because this was the way life would be for them in the United States for a long, long time.

So, it is in both America's and the European Union's interest to band together and find ways of reducing tensions between the Muslim and non-Muslim parts of their population.

Another problem is that there is still no "Europe" to negotiate with when it comes to foreign policy. Foreign and security policy continues to be the jealously guarded domain of each member state of the European Union, and this situation looks likely to remain so for the immediate future. Although it is true that the European Union is in the midst of trying to negotiate a unified European foreign policy and create a European foreign ministry, the success of this objective is far from assured. The European Union is a grouping of ancient, sophisticated nation-states, each with its own history of engagement with other countries in the world, and with differing perspectives. Until there is a unified European foreign and security policy, what is needed is a transatlantic organization that can serve as a platform to harmonize American security interests with those of the European Union to produce a consensus around the issue of rules of engagement. It would be prudent for Europe and America to think about a way to include the Islamic world's raw sensitivities in this initiative.

The final problem is the divide between the Republican traditionalists and neoconservatives. The neoconservatives still believe the United States has the remit to act as judge, jury, and executioner to determine the fate of countries deemed by them to be outlaw nations, irrespective of international opinion to the contrary. They want America to use its power to topple regimes and remake countries with a coalition of the willing if possible, alone if necessary, to spread freedom and democracy, even at the point of the sword. To these neoconservatives, an agreement on basic ground rules for the use of force with Europeans—with their preference for negotiations and multilateral institutions—is akin to tying America's hands. It will be virtually impossible to achieve this use of force agreement, the prerequisite for rebuilding a new alliance, unless the neoconservatives' decisive influence within the administration is reduced. While a number of the administration's more prominent neoconservatives have moved on, the path they have set this country on is still being followed, and their influence appears little abated. Hardly a day goes by without the American secretary of state making another speech about the need to spread democracy in the world, a strategy that is a key belief of the neoconservatives.

Negotiations for such a landmark agreement will not just happen. One side needs to take the initiative to start them, and that someone, in my opinion, should be the United States.

Ironically, Iraq may well be the catalyst that draws the erstwhile allies together again. I would propose that the United States ask for a meeting with the European Union at which it should seek European help in ending the war in Iraq. As tough as it will be, America needs to let the Europeans know that it realizes that its invasion of Iraq is floundering and it needs help. America also needs to let the Europeans know that the negotiations on this issue, and any others that might come up, will be handled as between equals, meaning the United States will henceforth deal with the European Union as an equal partner across the negotiating table, is prepared to share decisions for the future direction of the Iraqi war, Iraqi occupation, and future Iraqi government with the Europeans.

Is this a hat-in-hand approach? Of course it is. But is this necessarily bad? Let's look at where we are today. A recent estimate projects the cost to America of its Iraqi adventure as more than $800 billion, and counting; there is already talk of balkanizing Iraq, the American electorate is rapidly turning against the war. Who knows what new pitfalls the next few months will bring? What is there to lose by turning to Europe?

This approach has the added advantage of correcting what is, in my opinion, the damaging tilt of American foreign policy toward Britain. It will force Britain to work within the European Union, or stand apart all on its own. If it chooses not to be a part of the European negotiating team, it will have no place at the table. As I have mentioned before, the "special-relationship" between America and Britain needs to change to a "special relationship" between the America and the European Union. I realize that there are robust military and intelligence relationships with Britain that remain in the interest of both countries. Yet there are similar, albeit arguably less robust, relationships with other European states such as Germany and France that also remain important. Britain needs to be placed in a wider European context, as just one player among many.

The Europeans, on their side, will have to come up with a common negotiating position. Will they be able to do that? My hunch is they will. I do not for a moment believe that in the long term there will not be a common European foreign and security policy. It may take time, but they will get there. Who knows what this policy might or might not mean for the United States? Repeating former President Bush's admonition, "The Europeans are in the process of trying to forge a common understanding about security and foreign policy," he said. "So it's important for the United States to participate in the dialogue from the beginning, which will ensure that America is treated as the ally that it is and not a competitor."

To succeed, these negotiations will require Europe and America to agree on common rules for the use of force and will force the Europeans to come to grips with a common foreign and security policy.

Under what auspices should such negotiations take place? And how would the United States and the Europeans ensure these negotiations do not amplify the very real feeling in Muslim countries that this is another attempt by the Western countries to dominate the world?

My suggestion is to use NATO for this purpose.

NATO–Keep the Machinery; Change the Name and Mission

The North Atlantic Treaty Organization is a multinational entity that is already in place and ready to conduct business. NATO has reconciled American and European security interests successfully for over fifty years. Its charter was purposely written to permit it to expand membership beyond the number of countries that were the original signatories. It has gone through just such an expansion recently, to include its former enemies, the erstwhile Communist East European states, in its membership. It is the only organization that connects European states and America at the highest governmental levels and that has been used successfully to forge transatlantic consensus on sensitive issues for half a century. And most important of all, as we have seen, it is connected at the hip to the United Nations.

It also now happens to be on life support, looking for a new mission since the Cold War ended and robbed it of its primary responsibility–defense against the Soviet Union. It should by now be clear to even the most optimistic and nostalgic American and European that NATO's original mission is dead; America's perpetual leadership of NATO is dead; the use of NATO for military missions will continue to be an exercise in failure, given that the European and Americans are poles apart in their view on using force. NATO's use as a peacekeeping mission outside Europe, while well intentioned, cannot possibly succeed for reasons I have discussed earlier.

Even without a transatlantic consensus on what it should be used for, however, there is, on both sides of the Atlantic, respect and affection for NATO–the institution and what it has accomplished. "It is one of those apron strings which tugs on us and reminds us of what NATO stood for, and why those values are still important," Scowcroft said. A MORI poll conducted in Britain during the summer of 2002 for the German Marshall Fund of the United States[8] showed that 62 percent of Germans and 62 percent of the French (neither of whom were part of the "coalition of the willing" against Iraq) believed that NATO should be strengthened, comparable to the 66 percent who so answered in Great Britain. NATO still has the potential to serve as a powerful building block for the new alliance, but it needs to have a new mission with a relevant purpose, a purpose that it can fulfill.

With this kind of goodwill built into it, why not re-energize NATO by using it to forge a consensus on new rules of engagement? It may not square with the conventional wisdom about NATO's established mission, but that mission doesn't even exist any more, as earlier discussed. Who knows where this exercise will take the erstwhile alliance? A successful outcome could well be followed by a new NATO, whose mission, governance, and leadership are agreed to by the entire transatlantic community. And if its new mission is designed to accommodate Islamic interests as well, wouldn't that be a powerful, even decisive demonstration to the rest of the world of the West's conviction that the twenty-first century's power structure cannot work unless the sensibilities of a billion Muslims are taken into account?

Once NATO is demilitarized and refocused as an organization with the goal of building transatlantic consensus, it will also leave the Europeans free to develop their Rapid Reaction Force without the ongoing conflict with NATO's military mission. Perhaps in the future a new military role for NATO might emerge, a role in which the Europeans and Americans are again more comfortable with a formal defense arrangement. If such an eventuality does occur, the American side ought to be ready to accept European leadership of NATO if the cards fall that way.

Even more important, were NATO to facilitate agreement on the use of force, the new European-American relationship could well revitalize the United Nations and make the phrase "world community" mean something again.

Transatlantic Action to Make the United Nations Relevant Again

A new role for NATO is appropriate because it is rooted within the United Nations in both spirit and fact. Three of its members—the United Kingdom, France, and the United States—are permanent veto-bearing members of the Security Council. Like all international alliances, NATO owes its legitimacy to the charter of the United Nations. NATO's future is inextricably tied to the future of the world body. As a next step, Europe and America should collaborate in launching a project to make the United Nations more efficient and relevant to the new century's realities.

There was unanimous agreement among the leaders I spoke with that the United Nations is indispensable, but its administrative functions and the composition of the Security Council need an overhaul. All of the leaders felt that accomplishing this will not be easy because it is such a highly charged issue. Many countries—China, Brazil, India, for example— by virtue of their growing political power, economic power, and status in

the world, have every right to ask why in the world they are not permanent members of the Security Council if France and the United Kingdom, who are no longer major world powers, are? Virtually all of the
interlocutors felt Europe was overrepresented on the Security Council,
but they conceded that it would be virtually impossible to change the
Council's membership.

Might changing the mission of NATO and using it for the use-of-force
discussions under the umbrella of the United Nations increase the
chances of the Europeans agreeing to a reduction in their representation
on the Security Council?

All the leaders I spoke to realized that the relationship between the
United Nations and the United States had reached a new low. The
United Nations' recent "Iraqi Oil For Food" scandal, the examples of
graft and influence peddling, and a lingering feeling in Washington that
the United Nations tried to influence the 2004 American election against
President Bush, have ended any prospect that a report produced internally by the United Nations to improve itself will be readily acceptable
to the United States; and without American endorsement there is little
that can be done at the United Nations.

There was also a strong feeling among my interlocutors, however,
that although the United Nations should be critically analyzed, it ought
not be questioned as an institution.

"If you go back to the birth of the United Nations and the San Francisco
treaty," John Major told me (and I will let his voice represent the rest of
the leaders I spoke to), "Amongst its principal progenitors were President
Roosevelt and his successor Truman. Present at its birth were four or five
people who ran subsequently for the presidency of the United States. And
so the United States was very much at the core of the establishment of the
United Nations. In many ways the United Nations has been a bureaucratic
disappointment, but as a forum for solving disputes and for acting collec-
tively there is no substitute for it. Those people who think the United
Nations is useless and should be gotten rid of are very foolish; there is a
case for reform and efficiency of the United Nations, but there is not a case
for not having a United Nations," said Major. "The extent to which the
United Nations is efficient depends to a large extent on the member states.
If they provide it with the resources, whether cash or troops, it will be efficient, and if they don't then it will be inefficient."

Leave No Country Behind

Another potential magnet for transatlantic cooperation is the need for
Europe and America to immediately strengthen and coordinate the

process of ending the huge inequalities that exist between the have and have-not countries. Neither side can successfully do this alone. Europe does not have the resources, while America no longer has the world's trust or benevolent image to pull it off by itself.

To some extent the United States is moving away from a philosophy that has been very important for America: that its success and prosperity are not mutually exclusive with the success and prosperity of the rest of the world. The more prosperous other nations and regions are, the more prosperous America can be. "Poor nations cannot buy your products, they can't invest in your country, and poverty leads to instability and insecurity," Senator Hagel told me. "I think we are going through a time when we are starting to lose some of the sense that we need to bring the rest of the world along with us. It is important that we not only do that but it's perceived that we are doing that. The danger is, I do not believe that the rest of the world perceives us as doing that today. And, this spills over into our relations," he said.

What compounds the problem is that the reservoir of post–World War II pro-American goodwill has been largely drained. "Just take the demographics, forty percent of the people in the world today are nineteen years old and younger, they were not even born during Vietnam. They have no memory, no connection to what the United States did in the Second World War or the help it provided in rebuilding the world after the Second World War," Hagel reminded me.

Focusing on the inequalities between the have and have-not countries is a project that is tailor-made to galvanize the alliance. Between Europe and America, we have the money and technology to improve the standard of living of the rest of the world. Newspaper reports suggest that both Americans and Europeans are in favor of it. "This sense of solidarity with the rest of the world needs to be channeled and organized," said Paemen.

"Education ought to occupy a prominent position in this agenda," Scowcroft told me. "Terrorism, especially in the global al-Qaeda kind of manifestation, seems to come in part from the fact that if you look around that region from the Eastern Mediterranean up east to the borders of China, education is one of the most sadly neglected issues. What happens when the state education system is poor or non-existent? Religious education takes over, and it has been captured by extremists in the religion and used as a force of indoctrination," he said.

The United States and Europe together could help relations with the Middle East by developing an educational system that would be run by the people in the region themselves, but would be a vigorous modern education system developed and jump-started by the allies. "This is the best way in the long run to deal with al-Qaeda," Scowcroft said, "It gives us [Europeans and Americans] a long-term high profile engagement, for the best of reasons." Economic aid alone will not work in Scowcroft's opinion because, especially in the United States, "We haven't figured out how to do economic aid recently."

The 9/11 Commission recognized this need and recommended that "[t]he U.S. government should offer to join with other nations in generously supporting a new International Youth Opportunity Fund; money from the funds will be spent directly for building and operating primary and secondary schools in those Muslim states that commit to sensibly investing their own money in public education."[9]

Besides stability, security, and educational issues, the post–Cold War agenda for the European Union and United States must deal with the great human tragedies of poverty, disease, and despair. We live in an interconnected world of over six billion people where there are endemic health problems; SARS, AIDS, and the looming potential pandemic of avian flu are three recent ones. "They know no borders, don't discriminate between rich countries or poor countries. Poor countries are more vulnerable, but we are all vulnerable," Hagel said, "These are issues that have now expanded into the horizon of policy making and have the potential of bringing America and Europe closer together than we ever were before."

Dean Acheson, America's great Secretary of State, and his generation created a new world order from the ashes of World War II, an order that was largely successful in keeping the peace for more than fifty years. The epigraph of Acheson's memoir of that tumultuous time, *Present at the Creation*, quotes King Alfonso X of Castile, Spain (1221–1284): "Had I been present at the creation I would have given some useful hints for the better ordering of the Universe."

The European and American leaders of today have no such excuse; they are present at a time when the need for a new order becomes every day more apparent and urgent. They can and must take charge and order the universe for the twenty-first century—before it is too late.

Epilogue

It didn't work.

—William F. Buckley, Jr.

It was a telling moment when the *New York Times,* on February 19, 2006, published an op-ed by Francis Fukuyama, the noted Johns Hopkins University historian and author of *The End of History,* titled "After Neoconservatism." "As we approach the third anniversary of the onset of the Iraq war, it seems very unlikely that history will judge either the intervention itself or the ideas animating it kindly," Fukuyama wrote, adding, "There are clear benefits to the Iraqi people from the removal of Saddam Hussein's dictatorship. . . But it is very hard to see how these developments in themselves justify the blood and treasure that the United States has spent on the project to this point."[1]

I have argued in this book that the transatlantic alliance, which was already in intensive care, took a turn for the worse in 2003 with the United States' invasion of Iraq. In this misadventure, the neoconservatives played a leading role. Fukuyama had been one of the neoconservatives' strongest intellectual supporters until he refused to sign on to the invasion of Iraq. In concert with other leading neoconservatives, he had strenuously lobbied for the forcible removal of Saddam Hussein, first with President Clinton in 1998 and then with President Bush in September 2001. He had already begun to break with the neoconservatives when he refused to back the 2003 invasion of Iraq, and with this op-ed his break with the neoconservatives was complete.

Four days after Fukuyama's op-ed, William F. Buckley, Jr., the founder of *National Review,* a founding father of today's Republican conservative movement and one of its more thoughtful and erudite intellectuals, declared that the grand plan to invade Iraq, establish a democratic state, and remake the Middle East with thriving democracies "didn't work." He went on to say, "One can't doubt that the American objective in Iraq has failed. . . And the administration has, now, to cope with failure."[2]

Many of the neoconservatives that led America into the quicksand of Iraq are gone from the Administration now, but others soldier on in the faltering Iraqi cause, and their unwavering, almost messianic belief, that America can, indeed must, use its military, unilaterally if necessary, to push democracy into every corner of the world, and thereby gain brotherhood and peace for eternity still remains. Hardly a day goes by without either the President, his Secretary of State, or some other high-ranking administration official declaring that freedom is a God-given right for all people, and America is doing God's work in fighting for freedom around the world.

In the three years that it took Fukuyama and Buckley to reach their conclusions, over two thousand Americans and over a hundred thousand (no one really knows) Iraqis have been killed. Over $300 billion of American taxpayers' hard-earned money has been spent, and the end is not even in sight. The day after September 11 the entire world trusted the United States. Today, hardly anyone does.

"There was a time not long ago when we were accused of being simple-minded in the conduct of foreign policy, naïve and bumbling even, but everyone believed deep down we meant well, and acted ultimately with good intentions," Brent Scowcroft told me. "Now that goodwill is gone, nobody trusts our word or intentions, and it will take twenty to thirty years to bring that back again," he said sadly.

The imperial American adventure labeled "Operation Iraqi Freedom" was supposed to transform Iraq into a thriving liberal-democracy. A democratic Iraq would serve as the fountainhead of democratic thought throughout the Middle East. Instead of the Sunni-dominated regime led by Saddam Hussein, there would be a more representative government of elected officials from all corners of Iraq and from all its political factions. Islamic extremism would be curbed, and Americans would be safe again. Tragically, almost three and a half years later, the results are dramatically different, as The *Financial Times*' lead editorial on Friday, July 14, 2006, observed. "The invasion of Iraq broke the Iraqi state, fragmented the country, triggered sectarian war and proliferated jihadi-extremism." When I asked a Republican former high-ranking White House official whether he thought Americans were safer today than they were before the Iraqi invasion, his answer was an immediate and unequivocal "No."

It is worth going back to those heady and acrimonious days before the Iraqi invasion and to ask whether America and the world today would be a better place had the decision to go to war been required to be made in concert with our European allies. Hindsight has 20/20 vision, but in my opinion, had the Bush administration sought a true European coalition as his father had, there would have been no invasion. Even if, at a later stage, the allies had decided to go to war, consensus would have required endorsement by the United Nations. In either event, I believe, we would today have had a better and safer world—a far safer one for Americans—if the United States had marched in lockstep with its long-time European allies.

This is not to conclude that the Europeans were completely right, and the Americans completely wrong. (In a BBC interview right after the Iraqi war began, I was asked whether I believed Americans were from Mars and Europeans from Venus. I replied that I did not, but believed instead that both lived on Pluto and needed to come down to Earth.) There is nothing inherently wrong with the idea that America should always help other countries and people live better lives, to believe always in the United States as a Shining City on the Hill, and to extol the virtues of freedom and liberty. There will even be times when power is called upon to back up this belief. I contend, however, that the use of the massive military and financial resources of the United States in this cause will, for the foreseeable future, best be used through an alliance with the Europeans.

In the first two chapters of this book I argued that the present divide in the transatlantic alliance is different from the previous ones because the foundations of the post–Second World War alliance have crumbled and that, without analyzing this structural defect, it is futile to try and patch up the relationship. I later proposed (in Chapter 7) that the starting point for a new relationship is agreement between Europe and America on when and how to use force globally. The need for such an agreement and a new alliance becomes daily more apparent.

As I write this epilogue in late July 2006, not only are large numbers of Iraqis being blown up every day and the country appears to be at the brink of a civil war, but violence has erupted in another part of the Middle East—between Israel and Hezbollah in neighboring Lebanon. Rockets fly, civilians get killed, and there is real fear of a wider war that will draw Syria and Iran into the conflict. Neoconservative thought seems again to be in charge of America's foreign policy in the Middle East, as the U.S. Secretary of State revealingly described the destruction of large swaths of Lebanon and the resulting loss of hundreds of civilians as "the birth pangs of a new Middle East."[3]

Neoconservative voices are encouraging the American administration to use the "opportunity" created by Israel's retaliatory attacks in Lebanon and Palestine to teach Iran and Syria a lesson. "Why wait? Does anyone think a nuclear Iran can be contained?" asked the neoconservative *Weekly Standard.*[4] As was the case in the war against Iraq, facts do not seem to matter—no one has proved that Iran is anywhere close to making nuclear weapons.

Before too long, if Iraq is a guide, the rhetoric pushing for action against Iran and Syria will take on a momentum of its own, and a war that engulfs the Middle East will have begun.

George Will, one of America's best-known syndicated columnists, spoke to the senselessness of getting involved in yet another war, this time with Syria and/or Iran without coming anywhere close to winning any of the two wars—Afghanistan and Iraq—that are underway. "Neoconservatives have much to learn, even from Buddy Bell, manager of the Kansas City Royals" baseball team, Will said. "After his team lost its tenth consecutive game in April [2006], Bell said, 'I never say it can't get worse.' In their next game, the Royals extended their losing streak to 11 and in May lost 13 in a row."[5]

This new Middle East war provides an opportunity to demonstrate that America is willing again to move in concert with its European allies when it comes to using force, and begin the process of weaving a new alliance. As I write these words, meetings are being held with the Europeans to find ways to end the conflict. But they appear to be more show than substance—the American side having made up its mind to let its ally Israel continue the bombing campaign against Hezbollah no matter how many Lebanese civilians get killed in the process, and irrespective of what the Europeans feel. Hardly an improvement from the behavior the United States exhibited toward the Europeans during the run-up to the Iraqi war.

"Among real friends and allies such as the United States and the European Union and its members, things have a way of sorting themselves out," former president Bush had told me. My only quarrel with the words of this wise man, for whom I have the highest respect, is in calling Europe and America "real friends and allies." We are now barely friends, and certainly not allies, and we badly need to become so again.

Appendix A

The European Union and the United States: Transatlantic Drift or Common Destiny— Managing the New Reality

Conference held at Ditchly, U.K., April 11 to 13, 2003
(Organized by the Foreign Policy Association and ebizChronicle.com)

Over the weekend of April 11 to 13, 2003, twenty-two delegates representing business, government, and media interests from the United States and the European Union, met at Ditchley, United Kingdom, in a conference titled "The European Union and the United States: Transatlantic Drift or Common Destiny—Managing the New Reality," to discuss the state of the U.S./EU relationship and to bring policy recommendations to the table for helping to manage the relationship. The author of this volume was one of the directors (a list of participants is given at the end of this appendix). Our discussions were given added focus and urgency as a result of the recent damaging divisions between certain alliance members over the war in Iraq. We were fortunate in having a number of experienced transatlantic practitioners around the table and a chairman who combined a deep historical perspective of the questions under discussion as well as an awareness of the legal and strategic issues. We began by looking at the future of the transatlantic alliance from the cultural, business/finance, and foreign policy windows, but upon reflection we decided to add the cultural perspective to the other two and worked through two groups on Saturday.

Our discussions opened with an acknowledgment of the enormous changes to the strategic situation that had occurred following first the end of the cold war, then the attacks on 9/11 in the United States, including the recent American-led war against Iraq (American troops had just entered Baghdad that week). It did not take long for the group to voice the feeling that we stood in the ruins of the U.S./EU landscape. It was also felt that the European Union's Common Security and Foreign Policy (CSFP) was also in ruins.

The query, "How could a weak country such as Iraq cause such an upheaval not only in the transatlantic alliance but around the world?" became the thread that wound its way throughout the weekend's discussions. It was felt by many of us that Iraq was not so weak after all. Its importance lay in its potential oil wealth, the fact that it was an Islamic country, and its capabilities to develop and use weapons of mass destruction, all of which made it more powerful in the strategic equation than it at first appeared.

The root causes of the impoverished state of the transatlantic alliance were discussed in a direct and lively debate. According to some, it appeared that the European Union's quest for parity with the United States played a central role in producing the fault lines that had grown over the years and were simply awaiting a triggering event, which Iraq provided. The fracture, these participants felt, would have happened with or without Iraq. Others thought it was the role of France in actively lobbying the alliance in opposition to the United States, especially within the United Nations' Security Council, that began the downslide. Whatever the underlying causes, most of us agreed that this level of transatlantic disarray had not been seen before and that it had contributed to an unnecessary crisis, the effects of which may well be with us for some time. There was a good deal of broken crockery about, and the alliance seemed to the group to be on a very slippery slope.

Another area of lively debate was Iraq's reconstruction and its ripple impact. This action took place around the following points: Should the United States be forthcoming in sharing the reconstruction revenues with EU companies, and might this be a healing balm for the Transatlantic alliance's rupture? Would the refusal to involve EU companies cause a backlash from the European Union that might ripple into other world trade negotiations such as the Doha Round? What would be the role of the United Nations in the reconstruction as a catalyst for rebuilding trust within the alliance?

The participants also engaged themselves with a related issue: The old order had indeed changed and there was a need to create new rules to govern nations' behavior. Although it appeared to some that new institutions might be called for, it appeared to others that the practicalities of global consensus dictated the repair of existing institutions. An important point surfaced during this debate: The Eastern European nations joining the European Union don't necessarily look at issues only through an U.S./EU lens. To many of them, their role within the European Union is important in that they have recently been freed from the yoke of a dictatorial bloc.

The continuing Israeli/Palestinian conflict surfaced as another serious impediment to future EU and U.S. relations. Here we reflected the world outside, in that the formula to begin resolving it was before policy makers, but the political will to push it was not.

The group illuminated the deep commercial ties that bind the European Union and the United States: for example, over seven million Americans work for EU companies, and a similarly large number of Europeans work for American firms. It was felt that, rather than diverging, commercial depth and breadth had increased significantly over the last decade and the commercial links between the European Union and the United States were now greater by far than those in any other trade grouping in the world. It appeared to many of us that an information deficit existed between elites and the public regarding the depth of these linkages. One participant was vociferous in stating that ultimately people everywhere wanted to increase their wealth and standard of living, and this information deficit could well result in flawed policy making, thereby hurting the people of the United States and the European Union. Many of us felt that there was not sufficient dialogue taking place between business and lawmakers, both internally within the European Union and the United States and between them. Cultural overhangs appeared as an important differentiator for understanding the U.S./EU relationship. For instance, EU countries could never imagine 18 percent of their populations without health insurance, whereas the United States could never imagine living with 8 percent unemployment.

We reached agreement, however, on a number of important issues that are encapsulated in the "Agreed-To Message" in the next section:

Agreed-To Message

The Foreign Policy Association and ebizChronicle.com convened a meeting on 11–13 April at Ditchley Park on "The European Union and the United States: Transatlantic Drift or Common Destiny— Managing the New Reality." There was a very creative and constructive exchange of views between the European and United States participants. It was agreed that the Atlantic Community is vital to both sides of the Atlantic but that it is now under deep stress, which has been aggravated by apparently intensely held popular views which are incongruent with the real shared benefits gained from trade, investment and political cooperation. The group recommended that the United States convene meetings within the framework of NATO to take up the different perceptions of security threats, the different opinions of how to respond to them and the different capabilities of states to effect that response. The meeting also recommended that more accurate perceptions of the benefits of Trans-Atlantic economic relations be made available through revival of the Transatlantic Business Dialogue and other business forums. The Foreign Policy Association and ebizChronicle.com plan to continue their mission of public information about the relevance of foreign affairs to a vital American democracy by programs of publications and by convening further public meetings and conferences in the U.S. and in Europe on these urgent issues.

Disclaimer and Acknowledgment

This appendix, with the exception of the Agreed-To Message quoted above, reflects the Organizers' personal impressions of the conference. No participant is in any way committed to its content or expression.

The organizers acknowledge with thanks the assistance of IBM and J.D. Edwards in supporting this conference.

PARTICIPANTS

Chairman

W. Michael Reisman,
Myers S. McDougal professor of International Law,
Yale Law School (U.S.)

Directors

Noel Lateef,
President, the Foreign Policy Association (U.S.)
Sarwar A. Kashmeri,
Publisher & CEO, ebizChronicle.com (U.S.)

From the EU

Lionel Barber, U.S. Managing Editor, the *Financial Times*
Sir Nigel Broomfield, Director, the Ditchley Foundation
The Rt. Hon. Lord Howell of Guildford, opposition spokesman on Foreign
& Commonwealth Affairs, UK
Ferenc Gyurcsány, chief strategic adviser to the Prime Minister of Hungary
The Hon. Peter Jay, writer, broadcaster, former British ambassador to the U.S.
John B. Richardson, ambassador and head of the European Union delegation
to the United Nations
Robert Thomson, Editor, the *Times of London*
Mr. Hans Ulrich Maerki, Chairman of the Board, IBM Europe/Middle East/
Africa (EMEA)
Robert Worcester, Chairman, MORI

From the USA

Mahnoush H. Arsanjani, Deputy Director, Codification Division, Office of
Legal Affairs, United Nations
Mary Belknap, Vice Chairman, Foreign Policy Association
Jim Dougherty, Senior Vice President, Global Markets & Sales, Gartner, Inc.
Ivan V. Ivanoff, Executive Director, Richard C. Weldon Foundation
Brian C. Mck. Henderson, Vice Chairman, Merrill Lynch, Europe, Middle
East, Africa (EMEA)
Phillip Mills, partner, Davis Polk & Wardwell
Joseph Quinlan, fellow, Center For Transatlantic Relations
Emmeline Rocha-Sinha, Managing Director, MBIA Insurance Corporation
Jim Walsh, CEO, Capital Solutions LLC
William Tell, Jr., Chairman, William Tell Foundation/Texaco

Appendix B

North Atlantic Treaty, Washington DC, April 4, 1949[1]

The Parties to this Treaty reaffirm their faith in the purposes and principles of the Charter of the United Nations and their desire to live in peace with all peoples and all governments.

They are determined to safeguard the freedom, common heritage and civilization of their peoples, founded on the principles of democracy, individual liberty and the rule of law.

They seek to promote stability and well-being in the North Atlantic area.

They are resolved to unite their efforts for collective defence and for the preservation of peace and security.

They therefore agree to this North Atlantic Treaty:

Article 1

The Parties undertake, as set forth in the Charter of the United Nations, to settle any international dispute in which they may be involved by peaceful means in such a manner that international peace and security and justice are not endangered, and to refrain in their international relations from the threat or use of force in any manner inconsistent with the purposes of the United Nations.

Article 2

The Parties will contribute toward the further development of peaceful and friendly international relations by strengthening their free institutions, by bringing about a better understanding of the principles upon which these institutions are founded, and by promoting conditions of stability and well-being. They will seek to eliminate conflict in their international economic policies and will encourage economic collaboration between any or all of them.

Article 3

In order more effectively to achieve the objectives of this Treaty, the Parties, separately and jointly, by means of continuous and effective self-help and mutual aid, will maintain and develop their individual and collective capacity to resist armed attack.

Article 4

The Parties will consult together whenever, in the opinion of any of them, the territorial integrity, political independence or security of any of the Parties is threatened.

Article 5

The Parties agree that an armed attack against one or more of them in Europe or North America shall be considered an attack against them all, and consequently they agree that, if such an armed attack occurs, each of them, in exercise of the right of individual or collective self defence recognised by Article 51 of the Charter of the United Nations, will assist the Party or Parties so attacked by taking forthwith, individually, and in concert with the other Parties, such action as it deems necessary, including the use of armed force, to restore and maintain the security of the North Atlantic area.

Any such armed attack and all measures taken as a result thereof shall immediately be reported to the Security Council. Such measures shall be terminated when the Security Council has taken the measures necessary to restore and maintain international peace and security.

Article 6

For the purpose of Article 5, an armed attack on one or more of the Parties is deemed to include an armed attack:

–on the territory of any of the Parties in Europe or North America, on the Algerian Departments of France, on the territory of Turkey or on the islands under the jurisdiction of any of the Parties in the North Atlantic area north of the Tropic of Cancer;

—on the forces, vessels, or aircraft of any of the Parties, when in or over these territories or any area in Europe in which occupation forces of any of the Parties were stationed on the date when the Treaty entered into force or the Mediterranean Sea or the North Atlantic area north of the Tropic of Cancer.

Article 7

The Treaty does not affect, and shall not be interpreted as affecting, in any way the rights and obligations under the Charter of the Parties which are members of the United Nations, or the primary responsibility of the Security Council for the maintenance of international peace and security.

Article 8

Each Party declares that none of the international engagements now in force between it and any other of the Parties or any third State is in conflict with the provisions of this Treaty, and undertakes not to enter into any international engagement in conflict with this Treaty.

Article 9

The Parties hereby establish a Council, on which each of them shall be represented to consider matters concerning the implementation of this Treaty. The Council shall be so organised as to be able to meet promptly at any time. The Council shall set up such subsidiary bodies as may be necessary; in particular it shall establish immediately a defence committee which shall recommend measures for the implementation of Articles 3 and 5.

Article 10

The Parties may, by unanimous agreement, invite any other European State in a position to further the principles of this Treaty and to contribute to the security of the North Atlantic area to accede to this Treaty. Any State so invited may become a party to the Treaty by depositing its instrument of accession with the Government of the United States of America. The

Government of the United States of America will inform each of the Parties of the deposit of each such instrument of accession.

Article 11

This Treaty shall be ratified and its provisions carried out by the Parties in accordance with their respective constitutional processes. The instruments of ratification shall be deposited as soon as possible with the Government of the United States of America, which will notify all the other signatories of each deposit. The Treaty shall enter into force between the States which have ratified it as soon as the ratification of the majority of the signatories, including the ratifications of Belgium, Canada, France, Luxembourg, the Netherlands, the United Kingdom and the United States, have been deposited and shall come into effect with respect to other States on the date of the deposit of their ratifications.

Article 12

After the Treaty has been in force for ten years, or at any time thereafter, the Parties shall, if any of them so requests, consult together for the purpose of reviewing the Treaty, having regard for the factors then affecting peace and security in the North Atlantic area including the development of universal as well as regional arrangements under the Charter of the United Nations for the maintenance of international peace and security.

Article 13

After the Treaty has been in force for twenty years, any Party may cease to be a Party one year after its notice of denunciation has been given to the Government of the United States of America, which will inform the Governments of the other Parties of the deposit of each notice of denunciation.

Article 14

This Treaty, of which the English and French texts are equally authentic, shall be deposited in the archives of the Government of the United States of America. Duly certified copies will be transmitted by that government to the governments of the other signatories.

Notes

Introduction

1. David Frum and Richard Perle, *An End to Evil: How to Win the War on Terror* (New York: Random House, 2003), excerpted from pp. 247–250.

2. European Union, *The European Union: A Guide For Americans* (Washington, DC: Delegation of the European Commission to the USA, 2005), p. 2. http://www.eurunion.org/infores/euguide/euguide.pdf. Accessed July 20, 2006.

3. Lord Robertson, Secretary General, NATO, *The Role of the Transatlantic Community in Building Peace and Security*, speech delivered November 12, 2003, at the Conference on the Marshall Legacy, hosted by the George C. Marshall Foundation, the Center for Transatlantic Relations at Johns Hopkins, SAIS, and the Royal Norwegian Embassy.

Chapter One

1. Richard Bernstein, "For Old Friends, Iraq Bares a Deep Rift," *New York Times*, February 14, 2003.

2. Adam Bernstein, "Caspar W. Weinberger, 88; Reagan's Defense Secretary," *Washington Post*, March 29, 2006, Metro.

3. France waged a brutal but ultimately unsuccessful six-year war (1956–1962) to crush the Algerians' bid to end their country's status as a French colony.

4. "France, Germany Are 'Problems' in Iraqi Conflict," *CNN.com*, January 22, 2003. Speaking to reporters at the Pentagon's Foreign Press Center, Washington, DC, on Wednesday, January 22, 2003, Rumsfeld dismissed French and German opposition to invading Iraq by describing Germany and France as representing "old Europe."

5. In the September 2002 German elections, facing possible defeat, Schroeder formed a coalition with the Green Party and ran on a platform of opposition to any possible American military action against Iraq. He won a narrow victory. There were no congratulations forthcoming from Washington, DC.

6. Charles de Gaulle, "Europe and Its Role In World Affairs," speech delivered July 23, 1964, reproduced in Paul Halsall, *Internet Modern History Sourcebook* (July 1998). http://www.fordham.edu/Halsall/mod/1964-degaulle-europe1.html. Accessed July 17, 2006.

7. Joseph P. Quinlan, *Drifting Apart or Growing Together? The Primacy of the Transatlantic Economy* (Washington, DC: Johns Hopkins University's Center for Transatlantic Relations, 2003), Executive Summary.

8. Joseph Curl and Jeffrey Sparshott, "Bush Rescinds Steel Tariffs," *The Washington Times*, December 5, 2003.

Chapter Two

1. U.S. Senator Chuck Hagel, "Defining a Foreign Policy for the 21st Century," speech at the conference on "New American Strategies for Security and Peace," sponsored by The Century Foundation, *The American Prospect*, and the Center for American Progress, Washington, D.C., October 3, 2003.

2. Gen. Wesley K. Clark, U.S. Army (Ret.), *Winning Modern Wars; Iraq, Terrorism, And The American Empire* (New York: Public Affairs, 2003), p. 18.

3. Gen. Wesley K. Clark, U.S. Army (Ret.), *Waging Modern War* (New York: Public Affairs, 2001), p. 22.

4. Research conducted for the German Marshall Fund of the U.S. and the Chicago Council on Foreign Relations by MORI, UK, 2002.

5. Amnesty International, "Spain: ETA's Killing Campaign and Acts of 'Street Violence.'" http://web.amnesty.org/library/print/ENGEUR410122000. Accessed July 19, 2006.

6. Associated Press, "Terrorism Fight Top Agenda for EU Summit," March 21, 2004. Available at http://nucnews.net/nucnews/2004nn/0403nn/040321nn.htm#335. Accessed August 18, 2006.

7. Clark, *Winning Modern Wars*, xi.

Chapter Three

1. The North Atlantic Treaty is reproduced in its entirety as Appendix B of this volume.

2. Steven R. Weisman, "Fallout from Iraq rift: NATO may feel a strain," *New York Times*, February 11, 2003.

3. "Preparing to rebuild the international economic system as World War II was still raging, 730 delegates from all 44 Allied nations gathered at the Mount Washington Hotel in Bretton Woods, New Hampshire, for the United Nations Monetary and Financial Conference. The delegates deliberated upon and signed the Bretton Woods Agreements during the first three weeks of July 1944." Wikipedia, The Free Encyclopedia, "Bretton Woods System." http://en.wikipedia.org/wiki/Bretton_Woods_system. Accessed July 19, 2006.

4. Judy Dempsey, "NATO Chief Warns of Afghan Crisis," *Financial Times*, May 19, 2004.

5. Ahmed Rashid, "NATO's Afghanistan Troop Dilemma," BBC News, December 26, 2005. http://news.bbc.co.uk/2/hi/south_asia/4526150.stm. Accessed July 20, 2006.

6. Gen. Wesley K. Clark, U.S. Army (Ret.), *Waging Modern War* (New York: Public Affairs, 2001), p. XLIII.

7. Dean Acheson, *Present at the Creation—My Years In The State Department* (New York and London, W. W. Norton & Company, [1960] 1987), p. 284.

Chapter Four

1. Robert Kagan, *Of Paradise And Power: America and Europe in the New World Order* (New York: Alfred A. Knopf, 2003), p. 3.

2. For an excellent and detailed account of the French military involvement in Chad, codenamed Operation Sparrowhawk (*Opération Épervier*), see Wikipedia, The Free Encyclopedia, "Operation Sparrowhawk." http://en.wikipedia.org/wiki/Operation_Sparrowhawk. Accessed August 18, 2006.

3. Winston S. Churchill, "The Sinews of Peace," speech delivered March 5, 1946, reproduced in *NATO On-Line Library.* http://www.nato.int/docu/speech/1946/s460305a_e.htm. Accessed July 20, 2006.

4. The documents on the CSCE, or Helsinki Conference, can be found at *European Navigator*, http://www.ena.lu/mce.cfm; navigate to "European Organisations" and "Organisation for Security and Cooperation in Europe." Accessed July 20, 2006.

Chapter Five

1. I have drawn heavily from the late Professor James Chace's illuminating account of this weekend in his definitive biography *Acheson: The Secretary of State Who Created the American World* (New York: Simon and Schuster, 1998). The permission of the author is gratefully acknowledged.

2. I realize students of European history will rightly ask, "What about France and England, whose enmity was legendary and went on for centuries?" They are absolutely correct, but here the focus is on the twentieth century and especially on the aftermath of the two World Wars.

3. Chace, *Acheson*, p. 250.

4. European Union, *The European Union: A Guide For Americans* (Washington, DC: Delegation of the European Commission to the USA, 2005), p. 2. http://www.eurunion.org/infores/euguide/euguide.pdf. Accessed July 20, 2006.

5. Craig S. Smith, "Chirac Scolding Angers Nations That Back U.S.; 'New' Europe Bristles at Call for Quiet on Iraq," *New York Times*, February 19, 2003.

6. There are numerous sources for this episode. I have chosen to quote the article by Tim Weiner, "Word for Word: The Cuban Missile Crisis," *New York Times*, October 5, 1997.

7. Chace, *Acheson*, p. 249.

8. I realize that I am here open to the retort that the U.S. administration did not really follow through on the media headlines it helped generate—that is, it did not act forcibly in Darfur. That is a point I readily concede. But my argument still holds about bringing an issue to the fore if that is what the administration wants.

9. Peter Rodman, *Drifting Apart? Trends in U.S.-European Relations* (Washington, DC: The Nixon Center, 1999), p. 38.

10. I was host at a dinner reception for Lady Thatcher in 1997. Among the guests was a European Union official. During the question and answer period he made the mistake of questioning the "Iron Lady's" disdain for the euro. I am sure he will never, ever forget her slicing response. Readers will get a good idea of both the pro- and anti-euro arguments then prevailing in Chris Huhne and James Forder, *Both Sides of the Coin: The Arguments for the Euro and European Monetary Union* (London: Profile Books Limited, 2001).

11. Winston S. Churchill, "European Union," speech delivered September 19, 1946, reproduced at *Euro-Know.* http://www.euro-know.org/speeches/ paperchurchill.html. Accessed July 20, 2006.

12. David Fromkin, "The Importance of Being English," *Foreign Affairs,* September/October 1999, review of Ian Baruma, *Anglomania* (New York: Random House, 1999).

13. Dean Acheson, *Present at the Creation: My Years at the State Department* (New York: W. W. Norton, 1969), p. 11.

14. Ibid., p. 386.

15. *Foreign Affairs,* September/October 1999, review of Ian Baruma's book *Anglomania.*

Chapter Six

1. Daniel S. Hamilton and Joseph P. Quinlan, *The Transatlantic Economy 2005* (Washington, DC: Center for Transatlantic Relations, Johns Hopkins University, Paul H. Nitze School of Advanced International Studies), p. 16.

2. Joseph Quinlan, coauthor of the report cited in note 1, first taught me that the volume of exports and imports—the commonly used measurement for cross-border economic activity between countries—is a misleading measure for international commerce. Quinlan has for years now been convincingly pointing out that it is the total of two-way trade (imports and exports) added to sales of foreign affiliates, adjusted for potential double counting of affiliate sales and exports/imports, that provides by far the more accurate measurement. Underlying this concept is the idea that import/export statistics reflect a shallow form of economic integration between nations, countries are much more tightly bound together by their investment in each other. As Quinlan has pointed out more than once, Europe and America invest far more in each other than they do in the entire rest of the world.

3. Hamilton and Quinlan, *The Transatlantic Economy 2005*, p. 12.

4. Ibid., p. 6.

5. Ibid., pp 80, 81.

6. Manish Shah, "Fed, Dollar, and Gold," 123.com, April 22, 2006. http:// www.123jump.com/market-analysis/Fed-Dollar-and-Gold/17350/yes.

7. William Clark, "Petrodollar Warfare: Dollars, Euros and the Upcoming Iranian Oil Bourse," *Media Monitors Network*, archived August 8, 2005.

8. Carol Hoyos and Kevin Morrison, "Iraq Returns to the International Oil Market," *Financial Times*, June 5, 2003.

9. Clark, "Petrodollar Warfare."

10. "Iran Wants Oil Market in Euros," Associated Press dispatch in the *Toronto Globe and Mail*, May 5, 2006.

11. Hamilton and Quinlan, *The Transatlantic Economy 2005*, pp. 18, 19.

12. Samuel J. Palmisano, "The Globally Integrated Enterprise," *Foreign Affairs*, May/June 2006, p. 127.

13. Hamilton and Quinlan, *The Transatlantic Economy 2005,* p. 22.

14. See note 2.

15. Palmisano, "The Globally Integrated Enterprise," p. 130.

16. "Even fixed systems may use GPS, in order to get precise time." Wikipedia, The Free Encyclopedia, "Global Positioning System." http://en.wikipedia.org/wiki/Gps. Accessed July 28, 2006.

17. David Braunschvig, Richard L. Garwin, and Jeremy C. Marwell, "Space Diplomacy," *Foreign Affairs*, July/August 2003, p. 158.

18. Nick Cook, "War of Extremes," *Jane's Defense Weekly*, July 7, 1999. http://www.janes.com/defence/news/kosovo/jdw990707_01_n.shtml. Accessed July 28, 2006.

19. Ibid.

20. Braunschvig et al., "Space Diplomacy," p. 158.

21. "US Warns Against European Satellite System," *BBC News*, December 18, 2001. http://news.bbc.co.uk/2/hi/europe/1718125.stm.

22. Associated Press, "Europe Blazes Its Own Trail in Space, Riling U.S. Partners," *Space.com*, March 18, 2002. www.space.com/missionlaunches/europe_space_020318.html. Accessed July 28, 2006.

23. "US Warns Against European Satellite System."

24. "Europe Blazes Its Own Trail in Space, Riling U.S. Partners."

25. Braunschvig et al., "Space Diplomacy," p. 160.

26. "China Joins EU's Satellite Network," *BBC News*, September 19, 2003, http://news.bbc.co.uk/2/hi/business/3121682.stm. Accessed July 28, 2006.

27. Wikipedia, The Free Encyclopedia, "Galileo Positioning System." http://en.wikipedia.org/wiki/Galileo_positioning_system. Accessed July 28, 2006.

Chapter Seven

1. David Frum and Richard Perle, *An End to Evil: How to Win the War on Terror* (New York: Random House, 2003), p. 247.

2. Ibid., p. 48.

3. *Final Report of the National Commission on Terrorist Attacks Upon The United States*, Authorized Edition (New York: W.W. Norton, 2004).

4. Senator Chuck Hagel, "Defining a Foreign Policy for the 21st Century," speech at the Conference on "New American Strategies for Security and Peace," Washington, DC, October 29, 2003.

5. Reuters, "Schröder Rejects Military Force to Stop Iran's Nuclear Work," *The New York Times*, August 13, 2005.

6. "The United States and the European Union; Transatlantic Drift or Common Destiny: Managing the New Reality," Conference, April 11–13, 2003, Ditchley, England, sponsored by the Foreign Policy Association and the author.

7. "Public Opinion and Foreign Policy Survey," Research conducted on behalf of the German Marshall Fund of the United States and the Chicago Council of Foreign Relations, October 2002 by MORI, UK.

8. Ibid.

9. *Final Report of the National Commission on Terrorist Attacks upon the United States*, p. 376.

Epilogue

1. Francis Fukuyama, "After Neoconservatism," *New York Times*, February 19, 2006, op-ed.

2. William F. Buckley, Jr., "It Didn't Work," *National Review*, February 24, 2006, http://www.nationalreview.com/buckley/buckley200602241451.asp.

3. "Secretary Rice Holds a Press Conference," *Washingtonpost.com*, July 21, 2006. http://www.washingtonpost.com/wp-dyn/content/article/2006/07/21/AR2006072100889.html. Accessed July 28, 2006.

4. George Will, "Mideast Provides Refresher Course on the Limits of Power," *Valley News*, July 18, 2006, op-ed/syndicated column.

5. Ibid.

Appendix B

1. *American Foreign Policy 1950–1955 Basic Documents* Volume 1, Department of State Publication 6466, General Foreign Policy Series 117 (Washington, DC: Government Printing Office, 1957). Available at The Avalon Project, Yale Law School. http://www.cis.yale.edu/lawweb/avalon/nato.htm#art14.

Bibliography

I list here only the writings that have been of use in the making of this book. This bibliography is by no means a compete record of all the works and sources I have consulted. It indicates the substance and range of reading upon which I have formed my ideas, and I intend it to serve as a convenience for those who wish to pursue the subject of this book in more detail and to strike off on their own.

Acheson, Dean. *Present at the Creation: My Years at the State Department.* New York: W. W. Norton & Co, 1969, reissued 1987 in cloth and paperback.

Baker, James A. III. *The Politics of Diplomacy: Revolution, War & Peace, 1989–1992.* New York: G. P. Putnam & Sons, 1995.

Bush, George, and Scowcroft, Brent. *A World Transformed.* New York: Alfred A. Knopf, 1998.

Chace, James. *Acheson: The Secretary of State Who Created the American World.* New York: Simon & Schuster, 1998.

Clark, Wesley K., General, U.S. Army (Ret.) *Waging Modern War.* New York: Public Affairs, 2001.

Clark, Wesley K., General, U.S. Army (Ret.). *Winning Modern Wars: Iraq, Terrorism, and the American Empire.* New York: Public Affairs, 2003.

European Union. *The European Union: A Guide for Americans.* Washington, DC: Delegation of the European Commission to the USA, 2005.

Final Report of the National Commission on Terrorist Attacks Upon The United States. Authorized Edition. New York: W. W. Norton & Company, 2004.

Fromkin, David. *A Peace to End All Peace.* New York: Henry Holt and Company, 1989.

Frum, David, and Perle, Richard. *An End to Evil: How to Win the War on Terror.* New York: Random House, 2003.

Halper, Stefan, and Clarke, Jonathan. *America Alone: The Neo-Conservatives and The Global Order.* Cambridge, UK: Cambridge University Press, 2004.

Hamilton, Daniel S., and Quinlan, Joseph P., editors. *Deep Integration: How Transatlantic Markets are Leading Globalization.* Washington, DC: Center for Transatlantic Relations, The Johns Hopkins University and Centre for European Policy Studies (CEPS). 2005.

Hamilton, Daniel S., and Quinlan, Joseph P. *Partners in Prosperity: The Changing Geography of the Transatlantic Economy.* Washington, DC: Center for Transatlantic Relations, The Johns Hopkins University, 2004.

Hamilton, Daniel S., and Quinlan, Joseph P. *The Transatlantic Economy 2005.* Washington, DC: Center for Transatlantic Relations, The Johns Hopkins University, 2005.

Huhne, Chris, and Forder, James. *Both Sides of the Coin: The Arguments for the Euro and European Monetary Union.* London: Profile Books Limited, 2001.

Kagan, Robert. *Of Paradise and Power: America and Europe in the New World Order.* New York: Alfred A. Knopf, 2003.

Kupchan, Charles A. *The End of the American Era: U.S. Foreign Policy and the Geopolitics of the Twenty-First Century.* New York: Alfred A. Knopf, 2002.

Lewis, Bernard. *What Went Wrong: Western Impact and Middle Eastern Response.* New York: Oxford University Press, 2002.

Nye, Jr., Joseph S. *Soft Power: The Means to Success in World Politics.* New York: Public Affairs, 2004.

Patten, Chris. *Cousins and Strangers: America, Britain, and Europe in a New Century.* New York: Times Books, Henry Holt and Company, 2006.

Quinlan, Joseph P. *Drifting Apart or Growing Together? The Primacy of the Transatlantic Economy.* Washington, DC: Center for Transatlantic Relations, The Johns Hopkins University, 2003.

Reid, T. R. *The United States of Europe: The New Superpower and the End of American Supremacy.* New York: The Penguin Press, 2004.

Rodman, Peter. *Drifting Apart? Trends in U.S.-European Relations,* Washington, DC: The Nixon Center, 1999.

Weinberger, Caspar W. *In the Arena: A Memoir of the 20th Century.* Washington, DC: Regnery Publishing, Inc., 2001.

Index

About the Author

SARWAR A. KASHMERI has been recognized on both sides of the Atlantic as an observer and commentator on U.S.-European business and foreign policy issues since 1995. He is a Fellow of the Foreign Policy Association, for which he produces *Global Currents,* a bimonthly MP3 podcast, interviewing government and corporate leaders on foreign policy and business/public policy issues. He is a strategic communications adviser and business columnist and divides his time between New York and his residence in Reading, Vermont.